A VOTER'S VERSION

OF THE

LIFE AND CHARACTER

OF

STEPHEN ARNOLD DOUGLAS.

By ROBERT B. WARDEN.

"Wilde Stuerme, Kriegeswogen
Ras'ten ueber Hain und Dach;
Ewig doch und allgemach
Stellt sich her der bunte Bogen."

GOETHE.

COLUMBUS:
FOLLETT, FOSTER AND COMPANY.
1860.

FOLLETT, FOSTER & CO., PRINTERS, STEREOTYPERS AND BINDERS,
COLUMBUS, OHIO.

INTRODUCTION.

By a Voter's Version of the Life and Character of Douglas is intended here a history of that great statesman, drawn from all known sources of the truth, transforming into simple statement of the truth as apprehended much that is extravagant in other histories of Douglas, and dependent wholly on the vigor and beauty of the truth for its attractiveness.

The writer has been urged to undertake this version, not by a committee, but by voters as such. When the work was first suggested to him, he had seeming reasons for regarding it with strong repugnance. And he was not easily induced to undertake it.

To appear before the public, with whatever careful explanation, as the author of a Life and Character of Douglas, is to risk the imputation of an undue eagerness to figure as a politician. Reasons which the author need not here advance, make him especially desirous to avoid that imputation.

But each voter, as such, has a duty to perform at present, of which few have had examples. The approaching contest at the polls may be well described as an expected but a quite unprecedented trial of ideas, interests, and relations. Puerile attempts to ridicule this notion will not hide from thinking voters its entire agreement with the truth. In view of it, a voter who is thought to have it in his power to produce a version, such as that attempted in this volume, of the Life and Character of Douglas, is, perhaps, *obliged* to yield to such suggestions as were made, as already intimated, to the author.

Having so determined, the writer began to collate the accounts of Douglas, with a view to the intended version. As he more and more became acquainted with the *order* of events already known to him, and added to his knowledge of the early life of Douglas, the bare sense of duty grew into a pleasure. Now, he freely owns, it is a matter of *desire* to trace the outlines of the Life and Character of Douglas.

Prejudices marked the first acquaintance of the writer with the history of Douglas. Opposition to the "Little Giant" drew the author even into public prominence some years ago. And though, after that forever memorable and forever glorious twenty-second day of March, when Douglas faced the centuries with his self-vindication, prejudices fled from every discriminating mind, and he who writes this volume hastened with unnumbered others to acknowledge his correction, it was only in assembling the materials of this production that the writer began to take the true dimensions of the greatness embodied in the real life and character of Douglas.

In that real life and character is such an illustration of orderly developed strength, of constantly pursued design, of thoroughly elaborated great conceptions, as alone makes the historian proud in presence of his subject. Add to this, the exaltation won by an unfavored, young, and unimposing emigrant to a new scene of action, and you have such a life and character to contemplate as any writer may be happy to describe for any purpose. In the simplest history of the career of Douglas, and the least idealized conception of his character, we seem to penetrate the region of romance. And though no steed caparisoned, no burnished armor, no chivalric gallantry of any kind, appear, in the historic reproduction of the life of Douglas, gallantry of a far higher order here enlists our admiration.

But the reader must not fancy that the writer is in danger of forgetting his design to make a voter's—not a poet's—version of the Life of Douglas. While no stateliness of manner is intended, and while natural affection for the greatness manifested in the life and character of Douglas will be suffered its free play, this history shall constantly endeavor to support its title. I desire, and I intend, to lay before the public a true voter's version, as already defined, of the most interesting facts composing the career and indicating the proclivities of Douglas.

Such a version ought to be acceptable to all who mean to take the least concern in the approaching contest at the polls. It ought to be acceptable at the South, because in its agreement with the real sentiment of Northern States it cannot be "incendiary." It ought to be acceptable at the North because in its whole scope and spirit it is indisposed to any sort of novel doctrine, touching slavery or any other interest. It ought to be acceptable in every division of the Union, since its principles are those on which the safeguards of the Union ever must depend.

With reference, however, to certain very public, permanently uttered, unrecanted, and, perhaps, never-to-be retracted doctrines of the writer, it may be (locally) objected, that his version of the Life and Character of Douglas will be biased, sectional, illiberal, unfit to be addressed to South and North alike.

If objection such as this be hinted, answer may be found without offence to any, and yet with strict regard to truth.

The writer, then, in answer to the supposition of the possible objection, simply asks the Southern voter to examine all that follows ere deciding that this production is, by implication even, in fanatical contempt of constitutional considerations. Rightly understood, the record of the writer—carefully made up with reference to slavery—is equally remote from the fanaticism of the North and the fanaticism of the South. To justify this sentence may, hereafter and elsewhere, become the duty of the author. For the present, he contents himself with simply *stating*, that he never has been touched with the incendiary quality of anti-slavery opinions; adding, however, that even if the fact had been quite otherwise, he would now be ready to lay on the altar of the platform and the nomination made at Baltimore by the true representatives of the National Democracy, the offering of justly reconsidered views, of liberally moderated feeling, of an honest purpose to renounce all mere extravagance of all descriptions. If, therefore, from time to time as we proceed, the author fairly, freely, but respectfully remind our brethren of the ardent latitudes of things which they appear to have forgotten, and protest against their lately kindled scorn of things which all Americans should reverence, he will also testify, throughout, that the cotton flowers in the midst of noble virtues, and that the savanna and the prairie should be friends. While he discerns the evil of misunderstanding or of misbehavior at the South, he will not overlook the evil of misunderstanding or of misbehavior at the North.

The rush, the ever-varying excitement, the quickly altering conditions of a Presidential Canvass, do not often favor the production of a work like that here offered to the voters of the Union.

But no Presidential Canvass, of whatever date, could ever be regarded as a simple imitation of the Presidential Canvass that preceded it. Our people, and their objects of concern, are incessantly passing into novel and, to some extent, quite unexpected conditions and relations. Even their opinions alter, necessarily, with greater frequency and greater quickness, as well as far more radically, than a superficial view of our republican experiment would be able to reconcile with rational stability of character in government or people. There is always what may be distinguished, quite respectfully, as the unfixed or floating vote, and there are always partisans unable longer to continue their support of the party theretofore preferred by them. At present, many are in the just indicated case.

And there are also at the present moment, quite uncounted, even quite undreamed of, by the politicians, men who will permit no precedent declaration of opinion or of preference, no absurd pretension to consistency, no sort of selfishness, to keep them from the ascertainment, or to shackle them in the performance, of their public duty in this year of grace and plenty. Thus, it seems quite evident, that whatever may be done by way of preparation for November, all the calculations of mere politicians will be mocked when preparation shall have ceased, and the inevitable "It is accomplished!" shall reward the patriot or curse the plotter. Seek the most capricious of the winds, and you shall better calculate its courses than the changes which will end in blessing or in bale before the ides of March. The process of correction—self-correction—may be quiet, or the progress of fanaticism may be frantic. Decades of mere days may witness the extinguishment and the revival of the prospects now apparently the best, or now apparently the worst.

The considerations which I have presented seem to show that such a work as that here offered to the public, is not out of time. The declaration of one of our great men, that he had sworn upon the altar of his conscience, eternal hostility to every form of tyranny, is evidently applicable now to that self-tyranny, in which we sometimes mutilate the rights of conscience. No American is worthy of his rights to-day, if he permits himself to be a slave to that worst form of mental despotism, the pride of self-consistency.

There may be places, where deliberately fixed opinions, preferences, and associations, may be treated as unalterable. But in our America, all is experiment. We work out in our legislation, in our voting, in our public action of all kinds, the propositions that appear to us as principles of policy. We often find that we have been mistaken. Then, there is no time to lose. A single vote may make amendment of the error. Though we hear no magic " Presto! change!" we quickly move in the direction indicated by our wish of betterment.

However this may be in general, it must prove so at present. Here are interests inestimable exposed to peril. One ill-given vote may rend an empire. One ill-taken step may lead to ruin. One self-conquest may preserve the Union.

Sneers at views like these will hardly show their fallacy. If they are really absurd, then all the hopes, wherever entertained, of long-continued peace and union, are absurd. But no absurdity appears in them. Was it not true, as intimated on another page, that though not unexpected, the approaching presidential contest will prove quite unprecedented? Who will play the prophet now? Who ventures to predict the lesson of November?

"Here," it may be thought, "the writer is egregiously deceived. Although no man was ever really consistent, all men find it quite impossible to own that they were ever inconsistent. Even in the presence of the difficulties—poorly indicated by so tame a word—that now menace our beloved Union, few will act in such a manner as involves the evidence that they have ascertained erroneous tendencies in their previous political behavior, none will plainly own that they have errors to correct."

Such reasoning entirely overlooks the true distinction of the times. For years, it has been difficult, notoriously difficult, for any thinking, earnest, honest man to hold position with his party, be that party what it may. In politics, in medicine, and in religion, he who has not differed with his party, by open quarrel or by secret question, during the last ten years, has not thought at all, or has had differences with his conscience. These things are well known. And now the times permit such alterations of opinion as are alluded to in a preceding paragraph, and only the light weapons of ignoble warfare can be turned against a man who honestly avows that he has been in error, and that he intends to show his love of rightness by correcting his position.

Certainly, this disposition may itself mislead. If the present occasion called for any thing not plainly pertinent to a re liable account of Douglas, in his life and his opinions, the writer might, perhaps, admit that he himself has rather liberally used the right of differing with those who were in general his party.

In a certain view, indeed, of the design which animates the author of this little volume, it may not be deemed impertinent to glance in passing at the author's personal experience, with reference to doubts, and difficulties, and mistaken judgments, in politics.

The writer, then, is partly influenced to write this life of Douglas by the consideration, that he has with great publicity and not a little fervor, frequently denounced the hero of this history. Never satisfied with the provisions for the government of Kanzas, he is likely to continue in the notion that there was defect in those provisions. And he is not likely to become convinced that Stephen Arnold Douglas is to be acquitted of all blame, with reference to the unhappy four years, or nearly four years, following the passage of the Kanzas act, and preceding that redeeming day, when Douglas was himself again in presence of the Senate and the world. However this may be, the history of Douglas during those four years, connected as it seemed with the inaugurative anticipation by the President of the most unhappy *dicta* of the most unhappy judgment ever given in America—I mean the judgment in the Dred Scott case—induced the writer to believe, what, certainly, no honest mind can now pretend, that Douglas was an arch conspirator against the equal dignity, the equal interests, the equal rights, of citizens, who while they were not abolitionists, preferred free territory, and demanded that the people of each Territory should be really at liberty to have and to maintain a preference like theirs. It seemed to the writer that there was a general conspiracy, in which the Senator from Illinois was secretly at work, to bring about the judgment in the case alluded to, and to support its *dicta* under false pretence of obligation to accept them.

Nothing can be more entirely evident, than that the writer was mistaken as to Stephen Arnold Douglas. Nothing can or shall be more entirely hearty than the effort of the writer in this little volume to acknowledge, in becoming terms, the noble character of the self-restoration worked by that great statesman in the speech of March 22, 1858, and all that has succeeded it.

At the same time, as intimated, it is quite impossible to acquit our hero of all blame, with reference to the facts, in which there seemed to be a basis for the writer's now evidently quite erroneous judgment of the motives and intentions of the Senator from Illinois.

Indeed, among the reasons why it seems desirable to bring before the public such a history of the career and character of Douglas as the writer has attempted to produce, is the persuasion that most writers will be more embarrassed than this author in describing the unhappy period alluded to. From 1854 to 1858, the course of Douglas was imperfect, not merely as all human conduct is imperfect, but with reference to the entirety of which it was a part—in other words, with reference to all that went before it, and to all that has succeeded it, in the life of Stephen Arnold Douglas. While, therefore, the writer might be ready, were it pertinent, to enlarge the admission that alike in "bolting," as he bolted, and in the peculiar fervor of his bolting, he may not have been sufficiently considerative of the rights of others, he is clearly of the opinion, that a truly written history of Douglas will discern in the four years alluded to, the time of the eclipse of that great statesman. Glorious was the succession to that temporary hiding of his glory; but the fact of the eclipse ought not to be disputed, and in any veritable record it must be recorded. I will here record it.

I propose, therefore, with the permission of the reader, to present a view of Douglas which, perhaps, could not be presented by any one who has remained in constant and, as he would say, *consistent* harmony with the democratic party. I do not propose to trifle with the interests of Douglas—I do not propose to trifle with the real duty of a just historian—by lightly making this or that concession to the prejudices of the reader. Having ascertained the fair result of a true statement of the facts, I am prepared to make that statement and to offer that result to the intelligent appreciation of the public, as an ample tribute to the real greatness and the now unquestionable merits of our hero.

Part of the due preparation for the movements—nay, part of the movements themselves—which are to work redemption or to end in ruin next November, is the ceaseless critical examination of such characters as that of Douglas, to which this production is intended to yield some assistance.

Carefully remembering the obligations given to the reader, I propose to bring before the public in this little volume—sometimes by direct statement, sometimes merely by allusion or suggestion—all that I find to be notably involved in the taking of a fair and truthful view of Stephen Arnold Douglas, in his history and in his prospects.

Here, however, we must understand what may reveal itself to us in such an observation.

A fair and truthful viêw will doubtless find in Stephen Arnold Douglas, and his various experiences and performances, objects which cannot be spoken of in dry and strictly measured language. Nay, it is apparent at the outset, that a fair and truthful history of Douglas must be more or less a eulogy of Douglas. Being out of office, out of office-seeking, even out of that anonymous position in which one may have a certain greatness without official title — being, let me add, no court historiographer — I am not about to perpetrate precogitated praises of our "Little Giant." Yet I cannot, if I would, deny to Douglas the distinction which his history has made so precious in the eyes of all who struggle out of unexalted places into honorable prominence. It is evident, therefore, that fair and truthful as my work shall prove, it must be generally laudatory.

The varied, wonderful career of Douglas reaches back to a beginning, honorable but quite undistinguished. "Rough vulgarities" do not appear in that beginning, but there is no passport in it to the great distinction now enjoyed by Douglas. As our Western phrase would have it, here is no blazed way to eminence—the course is yet to be distinguished and the pathway yet to be cut out. The "Little Giant" is, emphatically, a man of the people. He has solved in his own history the problem of self-government. It is the boast of our political experiment and social venture, that from the body of the people, genius may arise to any elevation, private or public, favored by our governmental principles. We cannot credit Douglas, therefore, with the working of a miracle in rising to the height in which he is the favorite of admiration and the mark of envy. But the "Little Giant" can be credited with self-uplifting from an undistinguished way of life to a distinction not confined to any one division of the world. He can be credited, in explanation of this great success—success which no reverse of fortune can destroy, and no position much enhance—with traits of character which it is foolish to depreciate and vain to question.

He who speaks or writes of a career and character like these, will necessarily exalt his language, now and then, and never can be held to strictly measured applications of the terms devoted to laudation.

On the other hand, no real service will be done to real interests, if we do not, while tracing the career and ascertaining the distinctive tendencies of Douglas, constantly remember justice and discriminate the truth. Our sketch of that career, our indication of those tendencies, must be so clear, so free, so manly, that no question of its fairness can be fairly entertained by any voter.

Principles like these in a production like the present may be unfamiliar, but if they are new, they are not so in the sense of novelty as commonly objected to. At all events, I shall endeavor to observe them faithfully throughout the sequel.

Nothing more or less, it seems to me, will serve the cause of Douglas. For, I now begin to appreciate that greatness in our "Little Giant," which adopts as its peculiar cause, the interests of truth in general. There was, I own, a time when I could not perceive this in the character of him who is the hero of this history. But now I know, that I shall serve the cause of Douglas when I serve the cause of truth—that

Douglas not only does not need, but cannot well afford, to be misrepresented even by the partiality of his enthusiastic friends.

I have not asked permission to produce this life of Douglas. Looking on the "Little Giant" as among our public "institutions," I approach him for examination and description, as of right, and with the proud assurance, that I cannot injure, while I may appreciate, the object of my scrutiny. And there were reasons why I wished to be uninfluenced, untrammelled, unembarrassed, in the work here offered to my brother voters.

Let us pass, then, to a natural, unforced, familiar, yet so far as may be, accurate, account of the distinctions of our hero. Hero we may well permit ourselves to call him. His career has been heroic, and his heroism harmonizes with the tendencies of movement as our age devotes itself to movement. Brilliant, soldierly performances may not encounter admiration in his history; but great achievements in a scene of action in which splendid heroism may enact its wonders, will assuredly illuminate his record.

Forever as we view him, we must view the man. Political distinction, like aristocratic rank, is often

"but the guinea stamp."

But we may find the man revealed to us as Lawyer, Legislator, Candidate for the Supreme Political Distinction in America. Let us endeavor to discern the character of Douglas in the three capacities just mentioned.

THE LAWYER.

2

CHAPTER I.

THE STUDENT.

The genially written "Life of Lincoln," by our poet Howells, holds initially, and, as it were, platformically, that every American should have an indisputable grandfather.

If so, one defect may be at once alleged against this history.

There can, indeed, be no well founded doubt, that Stephen Arnold Douglas, himself, is quite free from such defect as that acknowledged as impairing this account of that distinguished statesman. Douglas, doubtless, has the usual supply of indisputable antecedents. But no grandfather is to figure in this history except the father of the Judge himself.[1]

It may be necessary, then, to look into the doctrine of necessity with reference to the particular here in question.

The supposed necessity is said to be, "in order to be represented in the Revolutionary period by actual ancestral service, or connected with it by ancestral reminiscence."

To display the absolute *necessity* of revolutionary antece-

[1] Since writing this chapter, and much that follows, I have examined Sheahan's Life of Douglas. But while I find sufficient evidence of the general proposition in the text, I find no named and therefore indisputable grandfather save as I have stated.

dents, in order to acceptability in the relation of the candidate to us voters, would require a more extended argument than the historian of Lincoln has devoted to that object. But, in sober seriousness, we Americans do hugely estimate the value of a set of revolutionary reminiscences in our incalculably numerous "first families."

For all that, candor here compels the plain confession that the evidence before the writer does not quite unquestionably prove that any remarkable infusion of the blood revolutionary filled the pristine veins of Stephen Arnold Douglas. Doubtless, however, this defect may be supplied. The gifted author of the "Life of Lincoln" "dimly intimates" (in imitation of Milton) more than he expresses, touching Lincoln's revolutionary antecedents. Now, why may not the fancy of enthusiastic Douglasites supply the possible original defect in the Douglas constitution?

But, however this may be, the author is unable, save by circumstance, to prove that the original ensanguination of the Douglas arteries, and veins, and capillaries, contained any indisputable infusion of the blood, that, classically, fought, and bled, and died, in the times that, classically, tried men's souls.

By circumstance, it may be sufficiently evident that the father of the mother, or the father of the father, of Judge Douglas must have been, if not an actor, then a warm well-wisher, of the revolutionary drama here enacted something like a century ago.

The fact that all the tendencies of the distinguished Senator to whom all eyes are now directed, are a little hostile to Great Britain, is familiar to the public. That these tendencies will undergo a mitigation in the Presidential office, may be well anticipated. But throughout the Senatorial career of Douglas, we have seen him strictly representative of the American, yet unsubdued hostility to England. May not this be suffered to establish, with *sufficient* certainty, that Douglas had an indisputable grandfather, and is thus connected, not merely by "ancestral reminiscence," but by "actual ancestral service," with the Revolutionary period?

But, seriously, let us follow from its known beginnings, the course of the Douglas antecedents.

All the sketches of these antecedents tell us, first of all, that Dr. Douglas was a physician well reputed, but not wealthy. It would seem, that though a native of New York, the father of Judge Douglas died at Brandon, Rutland county, Vermont. His death was sudden, being caused by apoplexy.

Of his personal peculiarities, his virtues or defects, presumption only could inform the writer, and it may inform the reader quite unaided by the author. It is not possible to the latter to give any accurate account of the distinguishing proclivities of Dr. Douglas. He will, therefore, only note the possibility that some not inconsiderable attribute of the distinguishing proclivities of Stephen Arnold Douglas may be due to his inheritance from one devoted to the service of the public as a physician. A physician is at once a public character and a near private friend of his patients, each and every. If he be worthy of his calling, he is one devoted to a sense of duty rather than to the entirely lawful ambition of winning a distinguished name. And though the little Stephen was but little more than two months old at the time of his father's death, no one acquainted in the least with the accepted law of antecedents will on that account entirely cancel the suggestion first submitted to the reader.

But no speculation of this sort deserves much space in such a record as this.

Nor can we permit ourselves to dwell upon the pleasant probabilities of the inheritance derived from the maternal source. The mother of Judge Douglas is not known to us by any, even the most insignificant, reliable account. The subject is too sacred for mere speculation.

Let us, then, content ourselves with knowing that the opening of that eventful history, which lies before us, does not seem without a notable relationship to the illustrious position to which its development has elevated Stephen Arnold Douglas.

On the 23d of April, something over forty-seven years ago, the history here outlined had its undistinguished commencement. How it passed through the developing varieties of childhood and the period of simple boyhood, we are little able to declare.

All that aids us here is information, that the widow Douglas, with the infant Stephen, and a daughter only eighteen months older, retired to a farm; that the whole of this farm was not the property of Mrs. Douglas; that little Stephen entered on the study of this world beyond the stinting, narrowing confines of city life.

If Douglas is what he appears to be, this is a fact of interest. If he is really and truly great—if he has worked a splendid way through formidable difficulties to a triumph which does not depend upon the question, "Who shall be our President?" —it is an interesting fact that he is not of urban origin.

Is it not the common voice of history that greatness seldom

dates from cities—from the Londons, Parises, New Yorks? Can any one regard it as an unimportant fact that Douglas had for birthplace and for place of first impressions, Brandon rather than Boston, Philadelphia, or Charleston?

The "Little Yankee," as the mixed æsthetics and fire-eaters of a certain region have begun to call Judge Douglas, was in his first years familiar with farm life in the vicinity of his New England birthplace.

In his time, the town of Brandon may have been quite different from what we find it now. Near the village passes Otter Creek, and Mill River, a branch of Otter Creek, is said to furnish good water-power. There are two cupola and two blast furnaces in Brandon, as well as a lead pipe factory, a last factory, a flouring mill, and ten saw-mills. But neither these, nor the adjacent railroad, nor the prized academy, nor the testifying thirteen schools, inform us largely as to the peculiarities of Brandon and its neighborhood as they impressed the mind of Douglas while it was most subject to impression. For we know not accurately how much all of this is due to changes of a recent period.

We are certain, that substantial old fashions more or less prevailed at Brandon in the boyhood days of Douglas. We are certain that the chief distinction of the progress then regarded by Brandonians was its tendency to better educational provisions, and to give a solid cultivation to the intellect.

How far the physical distinctions of the place may be regarded as reflected in the character of Douglas, it may be impossible for this historian to pronounce. At the instant of this writing, he has never seen the birthplace of our "Little Giant," and his information does not furnish him with the ability to give the reader more than a faint indication of the nature and the art with which our hero was familiar in his boyhood.

Otter Creek—a stream which in the West would bear a more pretentious designation—rises in the South-east of our hero's native county, flowing in a general course of N. by W. into Lake Champlain. Ninety miles in length, it is navigable for the largest lake vessels to Vergennes—six miles—and boatable from the falls of Middlebury to Pitsford, twenty-five miles. It has falls at Middlebury, Waybridge, and Vergennes, affording extensive water-power.[2]

Nearing but not touching Brandon village, it receives a branch which passes through the village, and affords good water-power for the local uses.

In its course, it once touches, and it generally nears, the Green Mountain region. When it reaches the vicinity of Brandon, it is still not distant from the mountains, and the landscape, of which it is part, is said to be a hill and valley modification of the mountainous vicinity.

The valley of the village is not wide, and the relief of inequality in surface, though not rising into mountainous sublimity or broken into glen or chasm, may entitle Brandon to description as romantically situate and pleasantly attractive. So, at least, the writer would infer from the descriptions given to him by a gentleman familiar to some extent with Douglas' antecedents, and acquainted well with Brandon and its neighborhood.

No feature of the landscape with which Douglas was familiar in his boyhood, and no feature of the social life that it

[2] Harp. Gazetteer, tit. OTTER CR., Vt.

contributed to fashion, strikes us with the sense of grandeur. But no moral meanness would reflect the *genius loci.*

Here we would not seek the flower of the virtues, which in latitudes of greater softness, richness, and variety, are thought to be indigenous. We should not seek at Brandon the peculiar charm of soft attractive graces, generous devotion to the promptings of a quick, magnanimous, chivalric spirit, easy and respectful interchange of various opinions. Whether we should find that charm, in its entirety, at present, any where within the reach of pro- or anti-slavery excitement, I do not propose at present to inquire. It is enough to know that if this charm was ever found except in the poetic fables, it is not to be discerned in Brandon now, and it was certainly not the distinction of our hero's birthplace during his boyhood.

On the other hand, there must have been at Brandon, in the times of Douglas, a considerable remnant of that puritan devotion to the sense of duty, which, when freed from foreign qualities, is certainly a valuable motive and an equally valuable check.

There were times in our brief history, when patriotic poetry and oratory well discriminated the sense of Honor as it ruled the then beloved "sunny South," from the peculiar sense of Duty by which the then esteemed New England was distinguished. Each of these distinctions once excited admiration, North, and South, and East, and West, throughout the Union. Now there seems to be a strange perversion, North and South. The sense of Honor, which has often beautified, now threatens to deface, the intercourse of North and South. The sense of Duty, which once constituted the security, now threatens to become the fire-brand, of the commonwealth.

But I will not anticipate. It is enough, at present, to remark that, in the room, equally of the perverted sense of duty which now manifests itself as mere fanaticism, and of the perverted sense of honor, which now attempts in certain regions to displace the Christian morals—the Brandonians in the time of Douglas acted with regard to a valuable remnant of the ancient puritan conception of devotion to the right.

That remnant had been freed to some extent from the alloying presence of some qualities, that sometimes seemed to make it a curse where it was meant to bless. And it is only fair to credit Brandon with assisting Douglas to a sense of right, which, developed freely by our Western boldness, freedom, and adventurousness, qualified him to command success and to despise any opposition that should attempt to arrest him by the false suggestions of the code of honor.

Language such as this is necessary to the purposes, which lie before the writer. But, unhappily, it is precisely such as is most liable to be misunderstood. Let me explain it, ere proceeding further.

I am not aware that any instance has occurred of a refusal on the part of Douglas to acknowledge the *duello.* Whether he was ever challenged, I am not informed. But, certainly, the course of his opponents more than once has looked in the direction of the duel. Northern minds, averse to any recognition of that species of conflict, which in other latitudes has been resorted to with freedom, as if it could settle principles or shield the right, have more than once been tempted to forget alike the morals which they reverence, and the peculiar *status* of the "Little Giant," by indulging for a moment the enquiry, "Will he stand this?" And intemperate discussions have been caused in Northern, and it may be in Southern circles, by the bearing of some Southern Senators towards the favorite of the Great West.

It pains the writer to refer for any purpose to the facts alluded to. From first to last, this volume is intended to reflect fraternal feeling towards all who honestly maintain opinions, moral or political, which to the writer seem erroneous. But the facts referred to—visible from time to time as *toning* Southern manner in the Senate-house, rather than in any noisily discussed aggression—are as much of interest to all true lovers of the Union as they are, unhappily, beyond the reach of question. And I should but ill perform the duty undertaken at the outset of this work, if I should shrink from the considerations here presented to the reader.

I must be at liberty, therefore, in several succeeding paragraphs.

Want of magnanimity and want of courage have been said to be discernible in the behavior, and to be apparent even in the original constitution, of our hero.

As our hero, Douglas must not lack a real magnanimity.

But the magnanimity which certain definitions of great-mindedness would designate, though not entirely wanting in the character of Douglas, does not seem to me a notable distinction of that character. Indeed, I may without offence to any place or person add, that with reference to received definitions, magnanimity is not a marked distinction of New England character. Whether it belongs to Southern latitudes, the lesson of November may assist us to determine.

The magnanimity that is reflected in a great devotion to a great ambition cannot be denied to Douglas. The æsthetic magnanimity that gracefully approaches and dramatically illustrates the sense of such devotion, does not seem to me characteristic of our "Little Giant."

Practical, devoted to his aims, a man of will and destiny, Stephen Arnold Douglas has not studied, and he was not born to illustrate, the showy virtue of which magnanimity is the received name.

Neither want of real magnanimity, nor lack of real courage, can be found in Douglas, fairly tried by his designs, his duties, and his conscious value as a representative man.

It would be quite absurd to credit Douglas with the knightly courage known as bravery. The startling clarion, the glancing sunlight, and the waving pennon, might not elevate his courage into that peculiar blending of an uncontrollable excitement with high purpose, which Napoleon, even, left for illustration to his marshals. But it is in strict accordance with the truth to say, that no man ever lived the life of Douglas as a craven, or encountered duty as he has encountered it, as one afraid of any human power.

Certainly, young Douglas may have learned from the Brandonians—I do not confine myself to the mere village—to distinguish between courage, purpose, and performance, on the one hand, and the shining qualities, on the other hand, that sometimes dazzle men into a foolish sacrifice of life, of trust, and of duty, where the menace answers argument, and the duel takes the place of demonstration.

In the circumstances in which Douglas has been tempted by the usages that sometimes bare the sword or aim the pistol in the seeming interest of honor, courage has been really involved in simple maintenance of the assumed position, at the peril of the unprovided personal encounter, or the greater peril of reputed cowardice. Never has our hero been *at liberty* to fight false issues in false modes. Never has he been without a trust, a purpose, and a destiny too strong for him or others to subject to the mad hazard of the barbarous field, "where honorable difficulties are adjusted."

All this would be more apparent, doubtless, if we knew the history of Douglas as we ought to know it—fully and from the beginning. I regret that I am not at liberty to call upon my hero for some indication of his boyish foretastes of the antagonism that he has experienced in manhood. But my purpose to collect my facts without the knowledge of Judge Douglas must be thoroughly approved by all considerate, right minded men. And now I must depend upon the facts presented to the reader, leaving, though not finally, the question of the courage and magnanimity of Douglas with this observation: The community of a New England village did not lack, when Douglas was a boy, a real magnanimity—it did not then, it does not now, and it will never, lack a real courage.

It has now become a mooted question, whether poverty oppressed the youth of Douglas, compelling him to abandon his desire of college life, and to become—prophetically, witlings have suggested and respectable humorists have hinted—a cabinet-maker.

But before we reach that question, we may well dispose of another.

Having lived, to some extent, a farmer's life until he left the hills and meadow lands of Brandon, Douglas might have split a rail.

But, did he?

O momentous, O unanswerable question!

Whether Douglas ever so contributed to ease, to taste, to comfort, to security, in the economy of agriculture, it must be acknowledged that no history records and no tradition intimates.

As if by way of compensation for the absence of the raillery involved in any popular account of Lincoln, we were long permitted to enjoy the sober satisfaction, that our hero had been useful with his hands as a mechanic, not as a diversion but as a necessity. It was so grateful to our feelings to consider that our hero had been pinched into performance as a common 'prentice, that we cannot easily accept the information, that our hero was set to cabineting by his mother, "simply to cure an overruling boyish desire to work in wood."

I cling to the received account. I insist on the poverty of Douglas. What! Are we to have our hero elevated into youthful comfort and exalted into a gentlemanly joiner, where we knew him as a common "'prentice hand?" Are we, the people, to be told, that Douglas loved to whittle, "peskily," and therefore was permitted to amuse himself and to exhaust his over-fondness for performances in wood, by *playing* 'prentice?

Seriously, the new story does not hang together; yet it may prevent some foolish errors, or correct some.

Neither pinching poverty nor an extremely opposite condition seems to have been known to Douglas in his boyhood. And we ought to be ashamed of caring much to count the widow-mother's dollars, on the day that Douglas "went to work" as an apprentice. Have we yet to learn that there are "rough vulgarities" in poverty and wealth alike? What great anxiety should we display to prove that Douglas did not choose, instead of being forced, to learn the art of cabinet-making?

If the fact is—and I know a shopmate of the "Little Giant" who informs me that it is—that Douglas worked at Brandon and at Middlebury—never "rowdying around"—addressing all his powers more or less to useful objects—to his trade and to his studies chiefly—if the local feeling, that each member of society should be an expert in some form of industry, at first led him to select, and if a growing preference of distinctively intellectual labor at last led him to abandon, the respectable mechanic art alluded to—whose pride is hurt, and who shall turn away from the career of Douglas with contempt or disappointment?

Doubtless, that would be an interesting history of Douglas which should trace him from the study of the fitness of things involved in furniture, to the study of the fitness of things involved in architecture of another order. Douglas, studying a joint in cabinet-making—Douglas studying a joint in legislation!—who shall paint this for us as it might be painted?

From the shopmate of our hero mentioned in a former paragraph, I have derived the information that the supposition which that paragraph suggests, might be converted into a historic statement. My informant is opposed politically to the "Little Giant," but he is an honorable man, now holding places of distinction in society, and he gives his recollections truly. If those recollections be not much at fault, the life of Douglas while he worked at Middlebury—remote alike from "rough vulgarities" and from the aimlessness that sometimes murders, as by a slow poison, all the hopes of youth—was the very sort of life which would prepare him well for the career before him.

Douglas, it would seem, though not a sloven, was, in youth, regardless of the great effect produced by dress. No lover of the beautiful will ever hold him blameless, and no lover of the economic can entirely overlook his fault, in this particular. When nature has not made us very beautiful, we ought to be a little economical of our good points.

It was the love of study, that made Douglas careless of his outward man.

And, after working out his love of whittling (or if better known accounts be true, after a certain loss of health had happened to him), unremitted study was the next experience of Douglas—study evidently ever since, in some form, the incessant occupation of this master-spirit—study, which in the academy, in the lawyer's office, in that Western emigration, in teaching school, in the "Squire's office," throughout the advocate's experience, upon the bench, in the addresses to the people from the "stump," and in the halls of legislation, might be varied, but could never be entirely given up.

The "rough vulgarities" which Pryor found in Douglas' early education, or its product, are not well apparent in the academic year at Brandon, or in that begun in Canandaigua, at the end of the Brandon school-days.

Mrs. Douglas having married Mr. Granger, Stephen went with her to Canandaigua. Here, as intimated, he entered the local academy.

The legal studies of the future Judge were also here commenced. But, although willing, I am quite unable to inform the reader by what course of reading, strictly legal or relating to the general development of his capabilities, young Douglas laid the strong foundation of his legal learning and his views of polity. I look upon it as a great defect in the accounts of Douglas, that they do not well possess us of his special preparation for the bar. Allowing all that ought to be allowed by way of discount on the rapid elevation of our hero to the office of State's Attorney, and afterwards to the supreme judicial dignity, in Illinois, I cannot but imagine that it would be well to know his course of study while in Canandaigua. We shall find in Douglas, as a judge, some evidence that he was really a student while in Canandaigua.

Having been, it is but fair to presume, quite cured of his Brandonian fancy for performances in wood, what was there in the new experiences of the future statesman to prevent his soberly preparing for the legal practice that so often, in America, prepares the Senator for Senatorial distinction?

Douglas never has been charged with the high crime of poesie. The gentle hills and lovely plains, the lake, the beautiful additions to the work of nature, in which Canandaigua is attractive, must have charmed the fancy, but they evidently did not poetize the character, of our law student. Blackstone was not necessarily a sacrifice to Byron, nor was Izaak Walton absolutely irresistible, because our student lived in Canandaigua. No: young Douglas must have studied—studied thoroughly—in Canandaigua. No such Judge, of any age, as Stephen Arnold Douglas proved to be at twenty-eight, was ever really a spendthrift of his time at the beginning of his legal studies.

Sheahan's Life—unknown to me when the preceding paragraphs were written—furnishes no indication of the legal studies in the office of the Messrs. Hubbell. But we are informed that our student, "on a thorough examination upon his whole course of study, was allowed a credit of three years for his classical attainments at the time he commenced the study of the law;" and that "when he removed to the West . . . . he had mastered nearly the entire collegiate course in most of the various branches required of a graduate in our best universities."[3]

In harmony with information elsewhere[4] noticed, I refer in this connection also to the Sheahan Life for an account of Douglas, in his boyish leadership in politics at Canandaigua. Douglas was a Jackson boy, and plead the cause of Jackson "like a man."

Of the peculiar political tendency of Douglas, I have elsewhere hazarded a judgment.[5] I will not at present dwell upon the indications, furnished by the "Life" alluded to, of Douglas, the best "posted" of the youths at Canandaigua in the politics of the time, the always ready for discussion, the accustomed victor in debate.

The reader must be eager to accompany our hero Westward. Nay, he cannot be patiently detained at Cleveland, with her inland sea, or at Cincinnati, with her

"wild and winding river,"

or at the City of the Falls, or at that great City of the Northern Mississippi, in which, as in Cleveland, liberal and noble men attempted to arrest the progress of our young adven-

[3] Sheahan's Douglas, 5.

[4] Chapter II.

[5] Written before encountering the Sheahan Life

turer.[6] Yet at each of these resting places of our hero, and on his way from point to point of his approach to his Illinois first impressions, trying ordeals, and great successes, much of interest is known to have occurred, and much of interest may be supposed to have occurred, by way of preparation for the greatness now developed in our "Little Giant of the West."

Was not that a useful sickness, which, at Cleveland, gave our hero time to study what he was and what he might become, and where he might apply, develop, and become distinguished in his conscious powers? If it sent him, weak, and "pale, and anxious," to Cincinnati, there defeating his desire of work by proving that he truly needed it—for so it is with our experience—if it deprived him of the buoyancy of mind that might have recommended him at Louisville, or made him hopeful at St. Louis;[7] it was still a useful sickness.

Stephen Arnold Douglas had been booked for Illinois.

> "There's a divinity that shapes our ends,
> Rough hew them how we will."

[6] "Mr. Andrews [Sherlock J.] was pleased with the youth; gave him all the information he could furnish, but advised him to remain in Cleveland, and as an inducement to do so, tendered him the use of his library and office until he should have pursued his law studies for one year within the State, as required by the laws of Ohio, when he would be entitled to admission to the bar, at which time, such was Mr. Andrews' liberal offer, Douglas was to be associated with Mr. Andrews as a member of the firm. . . . . Arrived at St. Louis, he made the acquaintance of the Hon. Edward Bates, then as now an eminent lawyer and an ornament to his profession. Mr. Bates was kind to the young stranger, encouraging him by his advice, and tendering him the free use of his office and library until he could get into practice on his own account." Sheahan's Douglas, pp. 7, 8.

[7] "He concluded to seek without delay some country town, where if his earnings were small, his expenses at least would be far less than in the large city." Sheahan's Life, 9.

CHAPTER II.

THE ADVOCATE.

Western emigration, including in its wild experiences even that precursor of the wilderness reclaimed, the steamboat voyage, must have made a deep impression on the mind of Douglas. Whether on the lake or on the river, steamboat life in '33 was full of various suggestiveness.

We may not be at liberty to entertain the fancy, that imagination, touched by new and strange realities, artistically "bodied forth the forms of things unknown," for Douglas, as he sat on deck or guard at evening to note and to enjoy the scenery of the "beautiful river." More reliable would be the fancy, that the morning with its golden promise strikingly appealed to Douglas on his western way. Yet more in harmony, perhaps, with all we know of Douglas is the supposition that the lively, varied conversation of the steamboat more and more prepared him for the working out of that "great principle," which Lincoln has learned how to ridicule, but which has been to Douglas as a guiding star.

The information which the writer has alluded to, as generously given by an early associate of Douglas, pointed among other things to the reality in all the being of our hero, of the tendencies that have devoted him to that great principle, which Lincoln only humorously affects to ridicule. For, Lincoln, let me say in passing, is what Lincoln is—no undistinguished dignity is represented in that statement—simply out of the reality and worthiness of that great principle. Whoever rings the changes on the words which designate the latter, in his heart confesses that they designate a grand, a noble interest of our humanity.

But, to return: The early life of Douglas, as it passed from honorable usefulness in a mechanic art into an equally honorable and useful preference of the pursuits which look to a professional and political career, gave testimony as it passed to a devoted sense of the great principle of popular discretion as involved in what we call the State. Apart from the expressions of his tendencies to be detected in the very progress of our hero towards public life, there are remembered more explicit declarations of the native tendencies of Douglas to accept with heartiness, and to defend and vindicate with constancy, the democratic principle of all our institutions.

And no mode of life, to which our hero owed impressions, previously to his adventure in the West, had in the least diminished his devotion to that fundamental principle. No portion of our country had been educated into an aristocratic estimation of "mud sills" or "rough vulgarities." No good or evil influence had made it lawful in the Senate, or discreet in editorial performances, to forget the dignity of honorable labor or to condescend towards unpolished honesty. And Douglas may have learned some lessons on those Western steamboats which conveyed him towards undeveloped Illinois, that have been, most unhappily, forgotten by his haughty or his condescending critics.

Steamboat life on Western waters at the time of which we write brought into friendly contact wonderful varieties of character. And conversation, in that life, was naturally full of our American ideas—of the farm lands to be cleared, of cities to be built, of navigation to be freed from peril, of the vast To Be in all its forms. It was, therefore, a school of our American philosophy in which the doctrines were alike acquired with readiness and applied with promptitude.

Of this philosophy, the whole career of Douglas is among the most instructive and suggestive illustrations thus far furnished by the history of American life. We have seen the young Jacksonian democrat as Mr. Sheahan pictures him, and as the gentleman before alluded to as having been acquainted with the youth of Douglas, has described his tendencies as then apparent. We shall find hereafter, that the *habit* of regarding all political and legal interests as popular in origin, in development, and in design and destination, sometimes quite unconsciously expressed itself in forms anticipative of the doctrines lately illustrated by our Senator. One instance will be prominently given in the next chapter. It will show our hero pointing out the *popular administration of the English Common Law,* when he had evidently no design of indicating his peculiar views of territorial conditions, rights, or interests.[1] And while we recognize the salient points of the life of Douglas as an advocate, we shall have reason to remark upon the constant interpenetration of his action and his views, by the

[1] See the notice in the next chapter of the opinion of Judge Douglas in *Penny* v. *Little*, 3 Scammon, 301.

omnipresence, if I may employ that word in this connexion, of popular rights.

Not only conversation on the steamboat — lake or river — must have tended to develop in the mind of Douglas the conviction just alluded to. His passage from the Forest City to Cincinnati was in part by way of the then so highly prized canal. The observations in New York, the encounter of the feeling in Ohio on the subject of canals and other public works, would have prepared him for a view of popular concernment in a system of improvements, in which more and more the omnipresence of the popular in our political experiment would be discerned by such a mind as we have contemplated in the Middlebury workshop.

Not to dwell too long in these considerations, let us once more fix our eyes upon the destination of our hero.

Illinois was not, when Douglas entered its domain of promise, what short-sighted politicians, with the view of meanly questioning the indications furnished by the great success of the lawyer whose career we now attempt to follow, have affected to consider it.

The State of Illinois has had a strange variety of population. First of all the European emigrants (or those of European lineage), came the French. We may hereafter glance at the evidences and influences of this Gallican feature in the settlement of Illinois, remaining at the time of which we write. And then a miscellany came, of which it has been easy to suggest the most ill-founded notions.

Even those who give us that account of Douglas, in which he appears as chosen, upon mere inspection, for the auctioneer's assistant, do not give a fair and truthful picture of the times. It is the implication of their anecdote, that Douglas had just penetrated into a western savagery. Now, though there were in 1833, and though there have been since, some portions of the State of Illinois, in which mere savagism was apparently predominant, it would be quite unjust to Illinois to overlook the leading character of the first settlements.

That leading character was very far removed from savagism.

No man can carefully examine the juridical and other public indications of the characters by which the settlers of Illinois were generally marked, without perceiving how absurd it would be, to consider all the State as we may fairly look upon some portions of it.

Jacksonville, where Douglas first proposed to "settle," had no savage population. Even then it had an educational distinction. Nor, I think, was Winchester, in which our hero played the pedagogue and (in the inoffensive sense) the pettifogger, a seat of whatsoever savagism then existed in the State.

It was, in general, in southern "settlements," that it was remarkable that there were "but few specimens of the more refined, enterprising, intellectual, and moral people," and that "society generally there was of a very low class." It was in Pope and Massac, not in Scott and Morgan counties, that the rogues built forts, and regulators took the powers of the law into unlicensed hands. It was not in the town of Jacksonville, or in the town of Winchester, that thieves and counterfeiters underwent the torture.

Doubtless, there are evidences that the evil of the lawlessness at first confined to southern border counties spread towards the North. Nauvoo was to the North-east of our hero's first "location." Joseph Smith and his savage disciples built their temple of abominations, set the State at naught, and met the bloody penalty of their trangressions in a region which was not at first distinguished by a savage disposition. Wonders are not seen alone in the diffusion of the anti-slavery and the pro-slavery fanaticism. All the forms of error are incalculably infectious.

At the time of Douglas' walk to Winchester, the Pope and Massac region had been under arms, and rogues and regulators—for the regulators had not then changed to rogues—had joined in battle, and the issue had been bloody.

How much Douglas knew and thought of these things as he journeyed towards Winchester, we know not. But if he was sometimes watchful on his lonely march—if with the iron will that bore him forward, struggled sometimes certain easily imaginable backward tendencies—who shall wonder? For, our hero could not have been wholly ignorant of the late bloody contest in the South of Illinois, and though he had selected quite another section of the State for his location, was he not a stranger, and alone, and who knows not the feeling of the lonely stranger in such circumstances?

On the other hand, the promises of Illinois were splendid, even as her realization of them has been.

She could show those fertile stretches between bluff and river, so remarkably productive of the only real "wealth of nations." She could show the only less productive regions of dry prairie land, in which the country has, perhaps, its best known characteristic. She could show her wealth of minerals for manufacture, her wealth of the facilities of commerce—lake and river and the open plain—her Mississippi and her Michigan. Her future was not evident, but all her promises were rational, and they were brilliant as well as rational. Though Springfield was a mere collection of log-cabins, and Chicago was but three years old, it may have been apparent to our hero that there was no reason for despair as he marched towards his destined first successes.

At Jacksonville, Douglas found some reason to be disappointed. Or, the state of his finances made it necessary for him to seek employment in some less pretentious place. His "rough vulgarities" now amounted to precisely 37½ cents.

It was not, therefore, mere preference of the Adamic style of traveling that moved him in that walk of sixteen miles to Winchester, "in search of a place" as teacher.

Nor was it a mere interest in auctioneering, which induced him at the latter place to play accountant to an auctioneer. The story here alluded to informs us that the future candidate for the Presidency pocketed six dollars for his "clerking" in this instance.

Here it may be seriously questioned whether any such experience as that alluded to was ever that of Douglas. For, the story tellers have it, that the auctioneer perceived that Mr. Douglas, who stood among the spectators, *looked* like a man who could write and keep accounts. Now, according to the rule of Dogberry, that "to write and read comes by nature," *some* men might have *looked* the mixed capacity to write and keep accounts. But Benton would have argued that the distance between the extremity of the superior garment worn by Douglas and the surface of the earth, was quite too short for such an indication.

So this anecdote, like the physical capacity of Douglas to be President, may be exposed to question.

But the walk is evidently no mere fiction.

What a walk that may have been! We have designated it a march. And march it must have been. And yet how every lengthened weary mile may have been marked by doubts and fears! In that adventure,

> "Remote, unfriended, melancholy, slow,"

as, partly, we may certainly declare it was, and, partly, we may well conjecture that it was, there must have been some thinking that would prove an interesting study, in the presence of the great success which Douglas has achieved. The weary way towards Winchester was really a glorious way towards Washington. But even the distinctive characters of Douglas do not warrant us in fancying, that an unbroken gladness marched with our adventurer, or that anticipation furnished him with brilliant prospects only, as he jogged on to the village where he hoped "to teach the young idea how to shoot."

It would be difficult to overestimate the proper dignity and usefulness of the schoolmaster's office, but it would be difficult to prove that, in that walk to Winchester, the attractions of the teacher's functions to our hero were remarkable.

He had not sought that Western State to win a place among the teachers, or a name among the educators. If he now desired a school, it was because he wanted money.

On the other hand, it was quite probable—nay, it is certain—that whatever melancholy musings, doubts, or fears, may have accompanied our hero, Will, unconquerable Will, went with him also. Else he had turned back, or at the least shown signs of faltering.

The modes of life which he had left were not the fashions of an ancient civilization; but between the way from Jacksonville to Winchester and the well-ordered town of Canandaigua, with its beautiful surroundings, what a contrast must have been presented at the time of which we write!

We have referred to Douglas as a man of courage. Courage must have been with him as he encountered the varieties of character that lay before him in that walk to Winchester.

I have, indeed, suggested reasons for accepting with allowance some of the accounts of early life in Illinois. And I have ventured to surmise that Winchester and Jacksonville were comparatively little marked by the contrasts to old-fashioned social life which certain parts of Illinois presented. But in no new State could the emigrant avoid encounters with the characters to whom the law of physical superiority is mightier than the law of the land.

How Douglas met these characters we do not know. But if he had not physical superiority, he had an intellectual and moral power that is greater than the might of muscle, that can aim with a more perfect skill, and strike with a more fearful execution—that does havoc where the strongest arms can only do a homicide.

We have no very reliable portraiture of Douglas dating so far back as '33. But then as now he must have had an armory with which he could encounter great apparent odds.

His popularity, so instant and so constant, moves our wonder. Yet why should it? Pithy sayings, forceful jests, strong answers and strong silences, were evidently at command with

Douglas from the first. And these are things which furnish few for the beginning of the race, and stay with fewer still to the conclusion of the contest.

Once arrived at Winchester, our hero's history began to show that tendency to public service—and, if the concession be demanded, to the honors known as public—by which the career before us is so notably distinguished. There is no paradox in stating, that the chief distinction even of the private character of Douglas is its public tendency or inclination. And this tendency appears to have been manifest at a very early age.

If Douglas, at the age of fifteen, had an overruling fancy for working in wood, his overruling fancy, at the age of twenty, proved to be to work in a material of quite another order. He began to show a disposition to be active in controlling mind, in mastering the difficulties of the public service, in furnishing himself with the capacity for statesmanship.

This disposition is not strikingly apparent in the teaching of those forty pupils at the town of Winchester. It may not strikingly display itself in the resumption of his legal studies, with the books borrowed from Jacksonville. It may not strikingly appear in his earliest forensic efforts—those of which his Saturdays were the appointed times, and which had for their humble forum the "Squire's office." But it is discernible throughout the whole career of Douglas from the instant of his first activity in Illinois.

When he was not quite twenty-one our hero was admitted to the bar, according to the liberal—the necessarily far from strict—provisions of the local system. His admission was in the Supreme tribunal—and within a year the Legislature dubbed him State's Attorney for the First Judicial Circuit.

To read the record of his rapid rise reminds us rather of the fiction than of the subdued and sober history of greatness

The "Life of Lincoln" already mentioned tells us, that the first recorded vote of Lincoln "against Stephen A. Douglas was on the election of that politician to the Attorney Generalship by the Legislature."

Doubtless—and I say it respectfully—the anti-Jackson feeling was so great with Mr. Lincoln that he *would have* voted against Douglas on the supposed occasion; and probably *did* vote against him for the less distinguished office already mentioned. But, if I am right, Mr. Douglas never was Attorney General of Illinois, and Lincoln never voted either for or against the "Little Giant" as a candidate for the place of Attorney General.

The esteemed author of the "Life of Lincoln," doubtless, followed what he found in cyclopædias, etc., in making the statement alluded to. And all the recent accounts of Douglas that I have seen, contain a similar statement.[2]

But on looking into the reports of adjudged cases, to examine what they might disclose of the peculiarities of Douglas as a lawyer, I discovered to my great relief, that there is probably an error in the statement in question.

Mr. Scammon, in the first volume of his reports, gives a list of the Attorneys General from 1819 to 1840. Mr. Douglas is not "listed." Nor is his name to be found as Attorney General in any of the reports.

On the other hand, there is a case,[3] in which *Stephen A.*

[2] New Amer. Cyclop. tit. Douglas; "Our Living Representative Men," p. 217; Life of Stephen A. Douglas, United States Senator from Illinois. With his most important Speeches and Reports. By a Member of the Western Bar, p. 22.

[3] *People* v. *Mobley*, 1 Scammon, 215.

Douglass—so his name is printed throughout the series of Illinois reports—appears as filing an information in the nature of *quo warranto*, in the capacity of "State's Attorney" for the "First Judicial Circuit."[4]

When I say that this discovery appears to me to relieve my hero from an imputation, I would not be understood as speaking disrespectfully of any office, past or present, in the State of Illinois.

But had our hero been Attorney General at twenty-two and with his slight experience, it would have been entirely just to charge him with a grave error at the very outset of his professional career. Indeed, I must be permitted to say, that a not unimportant departure from received ideas of a rational advancement was involved in the acceptance, six years afterwards, of the judicial office. And an error of the same description seems discernible in the first candidacy of our "Little Giant" for the Presidency.

It is quite in vain to answer these exceptions by appealing to the history of General Napoleon at the age of twenty-seven, or of William Pitt, the English minister, at twenty-four. The sober judgment of the real friends of Douglas will support the writer—speaking here with some slight reference to his own personal experience—when he concedes, that Douglas was too soon advanced to the supreme judicial dignity in Illinois, too soon advanced to the position of a candidate for the Supreme Political Distinction in America. Like Breckenridge, he was

"so wise, so young,"

[4] Since the foregoing was written, I have found that I am not mistaken. See Sheahan's Life, 21.

that we may almost wonder that he lives—that he has lived through all the trials of precocity to be entirely worthy of the honor which his party now with reason asks in his behalf.

But, unlike his æsthetically strong but not in other respects remarkably formidable contestant for the honors lately given in the Baltimore Convention, Douglas from the first and to the present hour has constantly been marked by an uncommon and distinctively substantial fitness for each place conferred upon him. If he erred in risking all the real perils and all the reputed evils of precocious public service, he so labored in his various relations to the public as to raise a question whether nature had not fitted him for all he undertook.

We know that nature never fitted any man for the performances by which the name of Douglas has been made illustrious. We know that Shakspeare's officer, already alluded to, was quite mistaken—that reading and writing do not come by nature. We are certain, that to be a lawyer is not born in any man, and that judicial honors, presidential dignities and trusts, ought not to be conferred upon a man before his ripe maturity of fitness.

If in nothing else, the course of Douglas now appears to have been erroneous in the particular here in question, because it has to some extent apparently invited that assault upon the now matured and eminently qualified "Senator from Illinois"—how many are there?—which accuses him of an inordinate ambition. I expect to make a full and satisfactory defence of Douglas against this assault. But on my conscience as a citizen, I dare not say that it was wise in Douglas to accept, so rapidly, the honors and responsibilities of which he has been so often the distinguished and successful bearer. And in presence of the pledges, given or implied in the initial chapter, I concede that he who votes for Douglas must excuse—he cannot justify, however he admire—the wonderfully rapid elevation of our hero, from place to place in political distinction.

But, however this may be, it seems to be conceded that our hero was remarkably successful at the bar. In itself this statement is quite credible: as a mere inference from the political advancement just alluded to, it would be only tolerable.

In '35 or '36, he represented Morgan county, and it may be, other counties, in the Legislature of the State, which ever since has generally manifested strong attachment to his fortunes.

Soon, however, he was appointed Register at Springfield. He resigned the place thus given him, in 1839.

In the meantime, when under twenty-five years of age, Mr. Douglas received a democratic nomination for Congress. In a district in which 36,000 votes were cast, the declared major ity against him was only five, and it is added, that "a number of ballots sufficient to have changed the result were rejected by the canvassers because the name of Mr. Douglas was incorrectly spelled."

Here as well as in the 1840 canvass, we encounter Douglas as a stump-speaker. Energy, directness, force, appear to have been manifested from the first in his performances as orator. His capability of work would also seem to have developed largely.

In the practice, strictly speaking, of the law, Mr. Douglas

is declared to have been notably industrious and notably successful. But of this I can present no very satisfactory demonstration.

Of the practice in unreported cases of Mr. Douglas, few memorials appear to have been made. And now,

"So doth the greater glory dim the less,"

there is but little disposition to possess the public of reliable and discriminating critical accounts of Douglas as a lawyer. We are told, indeed, that "he was noted, among other things, for the careful preparation of his cases, and for his tact and skill in the examination of witnesses. He never went into court with a case until he thoroughly understood it in all its bearings. His addresses to the jury were generally plain and clear statements of the matter of fact, the arguments logical and conclusive, and his manner earnest and impressive. He rarely failed to enlist the feelings and sympathies of the jury."[5] But this quite imperfect picture does not satisfy us.

While, however, this account of Douglas is unsatisfactory, it quite agrees with all the indications furnished by reported cases.

Lovett v. *Noble*[6] is the first *reported* case in which we find the name of Douglas as of counsel. It is followed by *People* v. *Mobley*,[7] in which our "State's Attorney" files a well constructed information in the nature of *quo warranto*, raising questions as to the authority of appointment and removal of clerks in Illinois.

In these cases, as well as in *Miller* v. *Howell*,[8] *Miller* v.

[5] Life of Douglas (Memb. West. Bar), 23.

[6] 1 Scam. 185.

[7] Ib. 216.

[8] Ib. 499.

Houcke,[9] *Covell* v. *Marks*,[10] *Whiteside* v. *Lee*,[11] *Spraggins* v. *Houghton*,[12] *Nye* v. *Wright*,[13] *Donnedy* v. *Bank of Illinois*,[14] our advocate is successful.

In the case of *Fields* v. *People*,[15] he is unsuccessful.

Some of the successes have relation to propositions in the law of pleading, some relate to evidence, and some to practice. All, so far as they reveal the part performed by Douglas, testify in favor of the view of his capacity, for which we are indebted to the "Life" by a "Member of the Western Bar."

Two of the cases mentioned have a special interest.

In one of them — *Fields* v. *People* — Douglas printed an argument; but I am not enabled to present his points. Mr. Sheahan tells us, that this "argument was regarded as so conclusive by the parties agreeing with him, that it was published in extenso in the papers of that day."[16] It is enough to note in passing, that the case presented a conflict between the action of the Governor and the action of the Senate, and that it was part of the movement, in which Douglas took a leading part, for a constitutional reorganization of the Supreme Court.

Spraggins v. *Houghton* merits a more ample notice.

In this case, not as an advocate presenting a mere question in the interest of a client, but, quite evidently, as a statesman advocating well-considered views of public policy, Mr. Douglas assumed the following positions, among others:

"It was the policy of the government by the Ordinance of 1787, and by the several acts of Congress for the government of the Territory Northwest of the River Ohio, to encourage

9 Scam. 501.

10 Ib. 525.

11 Ib. 549.

12 2 Scammon 211, and 2 Scam. 337.

13 Ib. 222.

14 Ib. 236.

15 2 Ib. 80.

16 Life, p. 40. See also the reporter's statement, 2 Scam. 81.

emigration, by conferring upon alien inhabitants the right of suffrage, and other privileges. Ordinance of 13th July, 1787, in R. L. 53, 54, permitting alien inhabitants to vote if freeholders."

"Fourthly. 1st. Under the Constititution of the United States, each State has the right to prescribe the qualifications of its own voters. Const. U. S. Art. 1, § 2; Federalist, No. 52, page 226; 2 Story's Com. Const. 57 to 66; 12 Cong. Deb. Part 1, 1036; Part 4, 4266.

"2d. Each State has exercised this power from the organization of the government. Book of Constitutions, Vermont; page 90, aliens vote and hold office.

"Constitution of New York; negroes vote. North Carolina permits free negroes and aliens to vote. 2 Kent Com. 61; 2 Story Com. Const. 58 to 65.

"3d. The naturalization laws have no reference to the elective franchise, neither conferring nor restraining it, in this country or in England. 1 Blac. Com. titles 'Alien,' 'Denizen,' etc.; 2 Kent Com. 61; 12 Cong. Deb., Part 4, 4246, 4247; 4 Harris & McHenry, 340.

"4th. A State may confer upon aliens the right to hold real estate, to vote, or hold office, etc., without making them citizens, or violating the naturalization laws. 2 Kent Com. 60; R. L. 626; (1) Book of Constitutions, 90.

"5th. The contemporaneous exposition of the Constitution by its framers, who were members of the Legislature, and by the different departments of the government and the universal practice under it for more than twenty years, has been, that alien inhabitants have a right to vote. Laws of 1819, Act regulating elections, of 1st March, § 14, page 93, prescribes the oath of the voter; 'that he has resided in the State six months.' No citizenship required; Laws of 1821, 76; same oath, no citizenship required; Laws of 1823, 58, §15; same oath, no citizenship required; Laws of 1825, 166, penalty for rejecting voter after oath taken. Laws of 1826 in R. L. 384 (1), inhabitants vote for justices of the peace.

"Laws of 1829, R. L. 246, 247, §12 (2), oath as to six months residence, but citizenship not required. All these acts approved by Governors Bond, Coles and Edwards, and the iudges of the Supreme Court, sitting as a Council of Revision. 1 Peters' Cond. R. 316, 317."

He was successful. The syllabus of the case is in part as follows: "Under the statute of the State of Illinois, every white male inhabitant, of the age of twenty-one years, who has resided in the State six months immediately preceding any general election, is entitled to vote at such election."

Here we may fairly meet the evidence, that while our advocate, as such, won great and well deserved distinctions, his proclivities were constantly towards political achievements.

If, indeed, the aims of Douglas, at the outset, had been merely those of a forensic taste and a propensity to strictly forensic service, it would be impossible to credit him with due devotion to his calling. But the destiny of Douglas was determined by the tendency, distinctively political, regarded by the writer as the most distinctive character of Douglas, view him in what light you will. With reference to such a destiny, the service of our hero at the bar and on the bench was quite harmonious with all his purposes and interests.

Indeed, with due regard to the inevitable obligations of the lawyer in America, how can he be indifferent to politics?

What right has he to urge the voice of ancient English wisdom as obliging him who serves the law to serve no other mistress? Is he not a citizen, a voter? If he knows what ought to be made known to the public, in respect to things political, what right has he to hide his knowledge from the people? If he does not know, how dares he vote in ignorance?

Our lawyers are, and must be, more or less conversant with political economy, or with that substitute for it, which parties organize to illustrate or to maintain. And so it would have been with Stephen Arnold Douglas, even if he had not been the destined statesman, whom we here attempt to view in all that evidently was contributive to make him what he is and what he may become.

But was the service in the Legislature—was the service as register—was the secretaryship—contributive to make our advocate a lawyer worthy of the name?

The full discussion of this question would be inappropriate in such a work as this. I must, therefore, content myself with saying, that I mentioned the facts just alluded to as part of the career of Douglas, and with no decided opinion as to their effect on his professional capacity. They may have favored that capacity—they may have prevented its development.

And so of the stump speaking. Some men learn the law while arguing before the people questions of great moment—some men lose their little law and gain no wisdom in its place while flying the American eagle.

Douglas, at one time, we are informed,[17] announced his purpose of a strict devotion to the law, in such a manner as to in-

[17] Sheahan's Life, 39.

dicate that he considered his antecedent devotion to political discussion and the like, an interference with professional ambition or with usefulness in legal practice. He became the partner, in 1839 at Springfield (where he had resided since 1837), of Mr. Urquhart.

But 1840 was before him, and he had no power to resist it when it came. It tore him quite away from his design of leaving politics. It played with him as with all others, like a storm-wind sporting with the strength of all defences set against it. All his prudent resolutions were as nothing when it came, to drive him into whirling currents of a vain activity.

The week of close debate at Jacksonville, the speeches at two hundred meetings elsewhere, were not wholly useless, for they largely contributed to save the State of Illinois to the State policy of the democratic party; but the cabin set on wheels passed over all resistance, a triumphant illustration of the power, but a melancholy instance of the madness, which may sometimes be the product of a false and foolish agitation.

Douglas went back to his clients, but he was soon appointed Secretary of State, and never afterwards has been permitted to devote himself to practice as he contemplated in 1839.

He was not destined long to play the part of advocate in the great drama of American activity. If he obtained distinction at the bar; if we shall find that he was afterwards distinguished on the bench; he still must be regarded as reserved for service in the Senate, and, as true hearts now believe, for a distinction even higher than his present dignity.

CHAPTER III.

THE JUDGE.

At the close of a recent speech, Senator Douglas humorously says: "I should not have much pride of opinion on the point of law, but for the fact that you have got into the habit of calling me 'Judge;' having among my youthful indiscretions accepted that office, and acquired the title."

No man can be readier than the writer to appreciate the indiscretion that may be expressed in a precocious judgeship. And the reader has already been possessed of certain serious concessions, touching the too rapid progress to judicial and to presidential honors on the part of Douglas.

But philosophy is often floored by facts. Without the slightest disposition to deny that in accepting the judicial office, at the age of not quite twenty-eight, Judge Douglas showed a "youthful indiscretion," I am forced to own, that this discretion did not manifest itself in the judicial *conduct* of our hero.

Practical; well grounded, as it seems, in legal principles; expert, it is said, and we have reason to believe, in the *art* of his profession; having studied in no unprofitable school the part of polity which must be part of jurisprudence; having mastered the political economy of the growing State in which he was to find the letter and to apply the spirit of laws—for such is the judicial function—Douglas certainly ventured, but surely he succeeded in his venture, when he solemnly engaged to meet the obligations of a judgeship.

If I have rightly indicated the peculiar duty of a judge—if this consists, substantially, in ascertaining what the *form* of laws apparently requires and giving force to the inherent *substance* of that form—the service of Judge Douglas as a legislator and his "first hand knowledge of the people," which if not derived was much developed in his "stumping," were among the useful preparations of our hero for his duties as a judge.

And so it happens that we must anticipate as we have often done in the preceding chapters. We must here take a view of Douglas as a legislator in the State of Illinòis, which the arrangement of our book would seem to hold entirely in reserve.

We do not, indeed, anticipate, but rather review, so far as chronological order is concerned, in glancing—for we can but glance—at Douglas as a legislator in the Prairie State. For it was on the first Monday of December, 1836, that Mr. Douglas took his seat in the Legislature of Illinois.

Speculation had bewildered Illinois. The last throes of the *monster* of contraction and expansion had apparently been felt, but little monsters followed with their mimic agonies, and speculative madness ruled the hour. Internal Improvement was the rage. The railway fever had set in—the canal interest still played no indistinguished part in the excitement of the times.

Mr. Sheahan, whom I do not quote but whose account I follow, gives a vivid picture of extravagance as illustrated at this period. He calls the session of 1836–7 the most important ever held in Illinois.

Mr. Douglas met as friends or foes—politically—Richardson, Hardin, Sample, Smith, Calhoun, McClernand, French, and Fields, together with that Lincoln who is now opposed to him—and well deserves his great distinction—as a presidential candidate. The name of Lincoln is not the sole tribute to the roll of fame which has been furnished by that backwoods Legislature, and the action in which Douglas, Lincoln, Hardin and the rest were actors in that Legislature was no child's play and no fool's diversion.

Douglas was, we are informed, personally opposed even to such propositions as the following: "1st. That the State should select certain leading and most important works, which should be owned, constructed, and worked exclusively by the State."[1]. He was personally not in favor of any system to which the State was to be a party. Yielding, however, to necessity as well as to instruction, he submitted resolutions, looking to a liberal yet moderate participation by the State in works of great utility. He failed, as any other democrat of *principled* or *constitutional* democracy would have failed, to tame the madness of the times. But he gave evidence of that political consistency, and order, and devotion to ideas, by which his career in general is marked, and in which a prefiguration of judicial wisdom is apparent.

Being chairman of the Committee on Petitions, Mr. Douglas yet more clearly manifested that blending of political sagacity

[1] Sheahan's Douglas, 29.

with juridical discernment which may be regarded as the very best qualification for the judicial office.

Henry King desired the Legislature to divorce him from his wife Eunice. On the reference to Mr. Douglas, of the petition, a report was drawn by the future judge, concluding with this resolution: "*Resolved*, That it is unconstitutional, and foreign to the duties of legislation, for the Legislature to grant bills of divorce." Mr. Douglas carried through this most important resolution, and, says Mr. Sheahan, "that was an end to divorces by the Legislature in Illinois."

On McClernand's resolution, disavowing the correctness of the charges made by the Governor of Illinois against the administration of Jackson, Douglas had a notable debate with the "gallant Hardin." But I do not point to this with confidence as illustrating the expansion of the mind of Douglas in the direction of judicial wisdom—for I do not know what was the point of the particular debate referred to. This, however, I will say with perfect confidence: Whatever, for a time, was Jackson's darkness, doubt, and groping mode of progress towards that unequaled system of democracy of which, towards the last, all recognized him as a new Apostle, reminiscent of Jefferson, no man could have been active in defending Jackson as our hero was, without becoming more and more acquainted with the system of democracy just mentioned. And no man could be acquainted thoroughly with such a system, without improving whatever in him looked towards capacity for the judicial function.

So, I undertake to say, it must have been with the discussions of our hero in debate with Hardin on the "stump."

To hold discourse of "stumping" is not quite agreeable to

certain sensitive, poetic-patriotic minds. I do not, as a Yankee would express it, "love" the word myself. But we may, if the fastidious be here irreconcilably at war with what is usual, express ourselves in some more chosen language.

Douglas, then, when he addressed the people in their free assemblies, was preparing the capacity, of which as we shall see hereafter the reports attest that he had become possessed when he became a judge.

"The first time," says Rev. Mr. Milburn, "I saw Mr. Douglas was in June, 1838, standing on the gallery of the Market House, which some of my readers may recollect as situate in the middle of the square at Jacksonville. He and Colonel John J. Hardin were engaged in canvassing Morgan county for Congress. He was upon the threshold of that great world in which he has since played so prominent a part, and was engaged in making one of his earliest stump speeches. [There it is again!] I stood and listened to him, surrounded by a motley crowd of backwoods farmers and hunters, dressed in homespun or deerskin, my boyish breast glowing with exultant joy, as he, only ten years my senior, battled so bravely for the doctrines of his party with the veteran and accomplished Hardin. True, I had been educated in political sentiments opposite to his own, but there was something captivating in his manly straightforwardness and uncompromising statement of his political principles. He even then showed signs of that dexterity in debate, and vehement, impressive declamation, of which he has since become such a master. He gave the crowd the color of his own mood as he interpreted their thoughts and directed their sensibilities. His first-hand knowledge of the people, and his power to speak to them in their own language, employing arguments suited to their comprehension, sometimes clinching a series of reasons by a frontier metaphor which refused to be forgotten, and his determined courage, which never shrank from any form of difficulty or danger, made him one of the most effective stump-orators I have ever heard."[2]

It is quite evident, that the "determined courage" of our hero served him well when he performed the duty of a circuit judge. In Mormon times and in the Mormon region, Douglas, it would seem, was often called upon to manifest the quality in question—once quite notably, in the appointment (not quite legal but most happily impromptu) of a Sheriff where there was no vacancy, and in assuming martial powers (witnessed by no governor's commission) in the room of mere judicial functions.[3]

Nor is it less certain that the "first-hand knowledge of the people," marked in Douglas by the Rev. Mr. Milburn, and the power, marked by the same observer in our hero, to speak to the people in their own language, must have been apparent as an excellency in the charges to juries made by Douglas on the circuit.

More than this: the judge, so saith the maxim, is the law speaking.[4] And the law, not in America alone, but—as Judge Douglas well observes (in effect) in *Penny* v. *Little*[5]—even in England, is the people speaking in and through the rites and forms of justice. So that in the State of Illinois, the law was in effect the people's voice. To be familiar with that voice, to be familiar with its modes of expression, to be able to adopt

[2] Ten Years of Preacher Life.
[3] Sheahan's Life, 50.
[4] *Judex est lex loquens.*
[5] 3 Scam. 304.

its common language, was, in circumstances such as those of Douglas, to be possessed of the all-penetrating spirit of the local legal system, and to be prepared for the interpretation and the application of the latter.

I would not be understood as saying, that to every man, or even to Douglas in all circumstances, that knowledge of the popular proclivities by which Douglas was prepared to be a judge, would be a preparation for judicial action. I would only say, that, having from the first accepted, not the sham, but the reality, of that radical democracy which is at the same time the only true conservatism in America, and having diligently studied Blackstone or some other elementary expression of English jurisprudence, Douglas, while engaged in legal practice as we know he was engaged, was well prepared for the judicial office by that intimate acquaintance with the spirit of the people, which, if I am right, and if my hero does not follow a delusion, is the real and efficient spirit of the law.

But, on the other hand, there are great cautions to be observed before agreeing that the whole of Douglas' antecedents fitted him to be a judge. This is a *Voter's* Version of the Life and Character of Douglas. And we have already seen that such a version ought to be discriminating.

It is doubtless true, that the peculiar tendency of Douglas leads him to *exalt* the sense of popular capacity. Our "Little Giant" has within him powers which forbid him to become a demagogue, in the offensive sense of such a designation. And whoever saw him as he stood, defiant, in the presence of ten thousand men, transformed by passion, at the instant, into quite ten thousand devils, cannot doubt that he is conscious of those powers.[6] On the other hand, a spice of demagoguery may be discernible in some of his performances. So it has been with all our statesmen—so it always will be, till perfection takes the stump or rules the Senate.

Tendencies of the description recognized in Douglas might have led him into most deplorable abuses of judicial power. But I cannot find that he abused in any sense the trust confided to him.

He was, undoubtedly, forever conscious of the duty which requires American judicial action to reflect distinctively American principles. And of these principles his view was ever broad and liberal. But while he understood the duty just referred to, and habitually took the comprehensive view just indicated, he had evidently studied philosophically—i. e. practically—that important rule of precedent by which the law developed in the courts of justice is preserved in its integrity and freed from that worst form of legal anarchy, caprice concealed in ermine.

Of the legal system which might be regarded as distinctively American, he has partly indicated his conception in these words:

"The common law is a beautiful system; containing the wisdom and experience of ages. Like the people it ruled and protected, it was simple and crude in its infancy, and became enlarged, improved, and polished as the nation advanced in civilization, virtue, and intelligence. Adapting itself to the condition and circumstances of the people, *and relying upon them for its administration*, it necessarily improved as the condition of the people was elevated.

[6] The allusion is, of course, to the attempted speech at Chicago in the autumn of 1854

"Is it to be presumed, then, that our legislature, in adopting the common law of England and the British statutes in its aid, prior to the fourth of James, intended to exclude all the improvements in the common law since that period? I do not wish to be understood as saying, that the act of the fourth George II., extending the right of distress to all kinds of rent indiscriminately, was an improvement; but I do say, that if we are to be restricted to the common law, as it was enacted at fourth James, rejecting all modifications and improvements which have since been made, by practice and statutes, except our own statutes, we will find that system entirely inapplicable to our present condition, for the simple reason that it is more than two hundred years behind the age.

"Why, then, it may be asked, did our legislature fix the fourth James I., instead of the date of the declaration of independence, or of the formation of our Constitution, as the period for transplanting the common law of England into this country? The history of our own country furnishes the answer. That was the period at which the first territorial government was established in America, and with it the common law of England as it then existed. From that period, we must look to American legislation, and the reports of American courts for improvements and modifications in the common law. In Virginia the right to distrain for 'any rent reserved and due upon the demise, lease or contract whatsoever,' was recognized by statute as early as May, 1730. The provisions of this statute, like our own, did not confer the right of distress; but recognized its existence, and regulated its exercise, in terms which clearly show that it was intended to apply indiscriminately to all kinds of rent certain. The district of country north-west of the Ohio River, including the present State of Illinois, was then within the territorial limits of Virginia, and in 1778 was organized into the county of Illinois. In 1783, it was ceded by the State of Virginia to the United States; and by the ordinance of the 13th of July, 1787, was erected into a territorial Government. That ordinance contains certain articles of compact between the original States and the people in said territory, which articles, it is declared, shall forever remain unalterable, unless by common consent. In said articles, it is provided, among other things, that the inhabitants of said territory shall always be entitled to the benefits of judicial proceedings according to the course of the common law. Did the parties to this compact intend to adopt the common law as it existed in England, before the settlement of America, or did they intend to adopt the common law as it then existed in this territory, modified and improved, and adapted to the condition, circumstances, and habits of the people, by a long course of American legislation and American practice? The mere statement of the proposition furnishes a sufficient answer. It was evidently their intention to secure to the inhabitants of the territory, the benefits of the common law, as it was then understood and expounded by the courts in America."[7]

This language, like the indication to be found in *Eells* v. *People*,[8] shows a lawyer-like appreciation of the conflict and the harmony of laws in our peculiar system.

In the case last mentioned, the decision in the court of last resort was not delivered until after Douglas had resigned his judgeship. But the case was tried below before Judge Doug-

[7] *Penny* v. *Little*, 3 Scammon, 304, 305.

[8] 4 Scamm. 498.

las, and the latter must have held in substance propositions such as these:

"The police power of a State embraces the power of regulating the whole of the internal affairs of the State, in its civil and criminal polity. The State of Illinois has power to prevent the introduction of negro slaves into the State, and to punish those of its citizens who introduce them.

"A State has the right to legislate on the subject of fugitive slaves, and that right is not taken away by the legislation of Congress on the same subject; but it seems, the States are prohibited from passing any law which may interfere with the right of the master to the services of his fugitive slave."

These propositions form a part of the *syllabus* in the reported case, in which Judge Shields delivered the opinion of the court. And we have the right to suppose that they agree in substance with the views of Douglas, whose decision was affirmed in the reported judgment.

These and other cases[9] prove that Douglas as a judge, appreciated principles in jurisprudence. Was he otherwise a judge in the full sense of that word?

The first report of a decided case in which Judge Douglas delivered the opinion is that of *Woodward* v. *Turnbull*.[10] The opinion is short, explicit, strong and clear. It is a case of statutory construction.

The next case[11] shows the same characteristics of mind. It is a case of statutory construction and of practice.

Stevens v. *Stebbins*[12] likewise manifests a plain, straightforward tendency of mind. It is distinctively American. It

[9] See, for instance the body of the opinion in *Campbell* v. *Quinlan*, 3 Scamm. 288.
[10] 3 Scamm. 1. [11] *People* v. *Town*, 3 Scamm. 19. [12] 3 Scamm. 25.

holds that in relation to variances, courts at the present day are not confined to the rigid rule of *idem sonans*, but, adopting a more liberal and reasonable one, enquire whether the variance be a material or immaterial one. The close of the opinion is: "If there be a material and substantial variance, it is fatal; otherwise, it is not. In the case now under consideration, we are of the opinion that the variance between *Steven* and *Stevens* is entirely immaterial, and consequently the Circuit Court decided right in permitting the vote to be read in evidence." [13]

In *Warren* v. *Nexson*,[14] the legal logicalness, clearness, and strength, which we have marked already, are apparent. We have also here a liberal, American, and lawyer-like appreciation of the rule of precedent. The syllabus, however, does not indicate all this. It is as follows: "If a plea begins as an answer to the whole declaration, and is, in fact, an answer to but part, it is bad on demurrer; but if the plea begins as an answer to but part, and, in truth, answers only part, and the plaintiff replies or demurs, the whole action is discontinued. Yet the plaintiff may take judgment by *nil dicit*, for the part unanswered, after replication filed and issue joined, at any time before final judgment, upon payment of costs." [15]

[13] A decision of like qualities is that of Judge Douglas in *King* v. *Thompson*, 3 Scamm. 184, in which the syllabus is: "A security for costs in which the Christian names of the plaintiff are abbreviated, is valid."

[14] 3 Scamm. 38.

[15] For a like indication of the characteristics of Judge Douglas as a "pleader," see *Dunn* v. *Keegin*, 3 Scamm, 292. See also *Townsend* v. *The People*, Ib. 326. And see *Davison* v. *Bank of Illinois*, 4 Scamm. 57. In the same connexion also may be read *Patteson* v. *Hood*, 3 Scamm. 152; *Carson* v. *Merle*, 3 Scamm. 168; *Dowling* v. *Stewart*, Ib. 193; *Gerrish* v. *Ayres*, Ib. 245; *Averill* v. *Field*, Ib. 390; *Fitch* v. *Pinckard*, 4 Scamm. 69; *Grubb* v. *Crane*, 4 Scamm. 155; *Gardner* v. *People*, 3 Scamm. 83. In some of these cases, the indication of Judge Douglas' views is only indirect. In one of them he merely assented, and in some his opinion did not harmonize with that of the majority.

In *Gardner* v. *People*,[16] Mr. Justice Douglas manifests the same reliable, simple, natural tendencies of thought. Many matters of mere practice were disposed of, and the following, which all my readers will be able to appreciate, is part of the opinion:

"If a juror has made up a decided opinion on the merits of the case, either from a personal knowledge of the facts, from the statements of witnesses, from the relations of the parties, or either of them, or from rumor, and that opinion is positive, and not hypothetical, and such as will probably prevent him from giving an impartial verdict, the challenge should be allowed.

"If the opinion be merely of a light and transient character, such as is usually formed by persons in every community, upon hearing a current report, and which may be changed by the relation of the next person met with, and which does not show a conviction of the mind, and a fixed conclusion thereon, or if it be hypothetical, the challenge ought not to be allowed; and to ascertain the state of mind of a juror, a full examination, if deemed necessary, may be allowed."

One of the most notable facts about this language is that it is, and professes to be, a simple copying of language used by Mr. Justice Breese, in *Smyth* v. *Eames*.[17] If Mr. Justice Douglas had been an absurd pretender, this mere "able copying" would not have satisfied his pride. For, then, as now, the public interest in the question to be determined was very great—and an absurdly ambitious judge would have aimed at an original "exfoliation" in this instance.

The case of *Sellers* v. *The People*[18] should be read with *Gardner's* case, just cited. On a fair comparison of the two

[16] 3 Scamm. 83. [17] Ib. 80. [18] Ib. 412.

opinions of Judge Douglas thus brought into juxtaposition, legal minds will recognize alike the justice of the views sustained by our jurist, and that of the writer's account of his judicial tendencies.

Here we close our view of Douglas as a Judge.

He was not faultless in that character. Perhaps the people would not love him, and perhaps the voter could not trust him, had he been a faultless character at any period of his existence. Sunday heroes—and I do not say this thing irreverently—are not for the service of the people in the Senate or in the White House. The people would be apt to answer Absolute Perfection as a Candidate for the Presidency, as Beatrice answered Don Pedro.[19] But be this as it may, our hero was not faultless as a judge. He is not faultless as a man. He would not, in the present state of things, be very human, if he were entirely faultless.

Seriously, it were idle to deny that certain faults of Douglas interfered with his complete performance of Judicial duties. But the fairly taken, and as fairly offered, specimens of his reported action as a judge which I present to readers, show in Douglas such a fitness for the judgeship, such a meeting and peformance of judicial duties, such a character in the judicial office, as gives warrant of his fitness for yet higher duties, and affords security for their performance with a practical, substantial, and reliable fidelity.

19 "*D. Pe.* Will you have me lady?

"*Bea.* No, my lord, unless I might have another for working-days: your grace is too costly to wear every day."—*Much Ado About Nothing*, Act II, Scene I.

THE LEGISLATOR.

CHAPTER I.

THE "MEMBER OF THE LEGISLATURE" AND THE "CONGRESSMAN."

WHILE treating of the various experiences which constituted the peculiar ability of Douglas as a Judge, we glanced at his legislative action.[1] With this glance we must content ourselves. The "Congressman" invites our scrutiny.

It is not my intention to be elaborate in the account of the congressional career of Douglas. The country knows the leading features of our hero's legislative life since he made his speech for the refunding of the Jackson fine. Whatever may have been the nature of his spell, he has been able ever since to draw upon his public action the regard of all divisions of the people.

But there is another reason why elaborateness is unnecessary in what follows.

If

"the child is father to the man,"—

if the effect can be determined by the cause—we know already what our hero is and what he must become. Have we

[1] Ante, p. 57.

not seen the opening of his career? Have we not marked his self-devotion in his youth to that divinely elevating labor, which, having once begun to make him useful in the public service, cannot cease to make him worthy of the public confidence?

But if it is unnecessary to be elaborate in the sequel, it may prove instructive to accompany our hero through the great temptations and enormous difficulties of his life at Washington.

It was in the spring of 1843, that resigning his judgeship, to which he had been elected by the Legislature, Feb. 15, 1841, Judge Douglas accepted his first entirely successful candidacy for the office of Representative at Washington. We are told, that he was advised, considering the doubtful chances of the election, to retain his judicial office, and resign it only in the event of his election. To his credit, he determined otherwise.[2]

At the time of his success, and during his service in the Lower House at Washington, our legislator was unmarried. But his triumph, after the prostrating sickness that succeeded the unprecedented canvass which with Mr. Browning had been made by Douglas, carried the latter "home again." Not forgetting by a stop at Cleveland to express his gratitude for the encouragement which had been given to him there, while, ten years before, he was wandering towards his destination, he hastened back to Canandaigua. An impertinent imagination would alone attempt to picture the unutterable pride and joy that must have welcomed him.

Our legislator took to Congress several securities against

[2] Sheahan's Life, 55.

erroneous action, several securities of largeness, liberality, American-ness, if I may be suffered thus to coin a word.

Against mere demagoguery, and for a truly popular, and therefore, truly representative career, his whole experience was a security. Occasionally—half in earnest, half in that often telling sport with the alarmists in which statesmen sometimes find it pleasant and not in any sense objectionable to indulge—our legislator might appear a little broad in his appeal to known popular preferences. But no demagogue was ever taught the lesson of Democracy as Douglas learned it—taking it to heart, and illustrating it in his own life, and feeling that whatever he had been, whatever he might yet aspire to be, he must attribute to democracy.

We must remember this as we proceed. For else we may find our hero more than once alarming us with something rather stronger and broader than we had expected. Nice effects for little genius—great effects for great abilities—this is the rule that seems to be developed by a careful study of the course and character of Douglas.

I have spoken of securities for largeness, liberality, a spirit truly American, which Douglas took with him to Washington.

He partly had them from the first of his experience as legislator, and they strengthened with his strength as that developed in the public service.

The population of the State to which our legislator has so often proved his usefulness and his devotion, was, as we have partly seen, derived from many sources. Douglas understood these sources and their various derivatives. The destiny of Illinois, like that of many other States, to modify the nationalities of Europe; or to reproduce their tributes to our popula-

tion in the transformation worked by a new scene of action, conflict, harmony; was evidently understood by him from the beginning of his course in Illinois. The remnant of the tribute sent by France to Illinois, the German tribute and the Irish tribute, as they were to be developed with the English tribute, tended towards the development of the ideas to which Douglas was devoted. And the differences of religious faith were placed in a strong light before him in that history of Illinois, to the materials of which his own career so much contributed.

A liberal, American regard of these varieties of national extraction and of religious belief—a catholic consideration of their unavoidable antagonism and their interest to harmonize without the sacrifice of principle—has from the first attested the fidelity of Douglas to enlightened patriotism and to true political philosophy.

Undoubtedly, this liberality of Douglas, this fidelity on his part to the constitution and the laws, this philosophic view of the inevitable future of America by which he has been marked, was due in part to the almost universal tendency of naturalization to enlarge the Democratic party. And the presence of our hero in the State and National Legislatures was undoubtedly largely due to the naturalized citizens of his district.

After he had been in the State Legislature, Douglas, as we have already seen, was active in procuring a decision whereby the established policy of Illinois was saved from a judicial sentence of destruction. In the case of *Spraggins* v. *Houghton*, noticed in a former chapter, he defended the established policy of Illinois to give the right to vote to every free white male

inhabitant above the age of twenty-one years. And the views expressed in his capacity as advocate were otherwise avowed, proclaimed, and propagated.

As for the religious views of Douglas either while he was a "member of the Legislature" in the State of his adoption, or since that time, I have only to say: I do not know them. Probably, they were more distinctively political than religious. From whatever cause, our public men have frequently displayed religious feeling rather in their tenderness and reverence towards the conscientious views of others, than in any well developed doctrinal professions or even preferences. Of the only Christianity apparent in the lives of many statesmen, the sole principle would sometimes seem to be: Blessed are the people, for they are the source of power.

This, however, I do not believe of Douglas. He has ever known the art of minding his own business, — in other words, he has always been capable of silence where he chose not to be noisy—and I am not in the least informed with reference to his religious views. But I imagine that his creed would have such articles as these: All men have a political, because they have a natural, right to be or not to be of any given church. It is the policy of human laws to free, and so to favor, conscientiousness. Beyond the limit of necessity, the State should not express as law disputed rules of conduct. Catholic and Protestant alike may safely be entrusted with the right to vote, and so may even all who own themselves non-Christian. No religious test should be permitted.

Views like these—and I am certain that they are the views of Douglas—my imagination here has all the force of absolute conviction — fitted Douglas, and they qualify him now, to be the representative of true American ideas. Elevating and refining in their influence, their simple entertainment opens all the mysteries of policy to comprehension. He who is precisely right with reference to fundamental interests like those alluded to, cannot be long without the key to all the difficulties of political economy; while he who is illiberal in this respect can hardly be a statesman worthy of the name.

A subject in which Illinois had an especial interest was that to which our legislator gave his first attention. His first speech—I do not call it his maiden speech—there seems no fitness in that term when Douglas is in question—always the opponent of our hero needed warning such as that which Scott addresses to Fitz-James:

> "Now, gallant Saxon! hold thine own—
> No maiden arm is round thee thrown"—

the first speech of Douglas gave a foretaste of his lasting interest in practical, important questions. It related to Internal Improvements.

Our Congressman, on the 19th day of December, 1843, insisted on his motion to refer to a select committee so much of the President's message as referred to the improvement of western lakes and harbors.

Mr. Douglas insisted on such a reference, "because the question involved important interests requiring an accurate knowledge of the condition of the country, its navigable streams, and the obstructions to be removed. A thorough examination of subjects so various, extensive and intricate, and requiring so much patient labor and toil, could not be expected from those who reside at a great distance. He desired a full, elaborate, and detailed report from those whose local positions would stimulate them. Let this be granted, and the friends of the measure would be content to leave its policy and propriety to the judgment of the House."

How far deeper insight, greater knowledge of the dangers which beset a legislative body in providing for public works, in a word, enlarged capacity to deal with the important interest to which our legislator gave his first attention, modified the views of Douglas as to Internal Improvements, we shall see hereafter.

Not in reference to this concern of public policy alone has time been useful to our Congressman. He was and is a teachable as well as an instructed politician. He was not "fenced in," when he was sent to Washington in '43.

The speech of Douglas for refunding Jackson's fine deserved the thanks of Jackson. And it was not unrewarded. Jackson is reported to have thanked our orator in person, and to have preserved the speech itself with singular honor. Time has had no work to do upon this effort. All its warmth is natural, and its extravagance, if any be detected in it, is of such an order as is always lawful to the orator who pleads for gratitude and worships greatness.

But when Douglas argues for the famous "54° 40′ or a fight," there may be a little room to thank the lapse of time which has been good to Douglas as it always is to an expanding genius for affairs. Our hero thus expressed himself in 1844:

"It therefore becomes us to put this nation in a state of defence; and when we are told that this will lead to war, all I have to say is this: violate no treaty stipulations, nor any principle of the law of nations; preserve the honor and integrity of the country, but, at the same time, assert our right to the last inch, and then, if war comes, let it come. We may regret the necessity which produced it, but when it does come, I would administer to our citizens Hannibal's oath of eternal enmity, and not terminate the war until the question was settled forever. I would blot out the lines on the map which now mark our national boundaries on this continent, and make the area of liberty as broad as the continent itself."

Like language was employed by Douglas in his speech on Texan Annexation. Thus:

"Our federal system is admirably adapted to the whole continent: and while I would not violate the laws of nations, nor treaty stipulations, nor in any manner tarnish the national honor, I would exert all legal and honorable means to drive Great Britain, and the last vestiges of royal authority, from the continent of North America, and extend the limits of the Republic from ocean to ocean. I would make this an ocean-bound Republic, and have no more disputes about red lines on maps."

Language such as this may be considered as requiring moderation. Can it be regarded as objectionable as tending to a spirit of encroachment?

Let no answer be attempted to this question, save with reference to the ideas which throughout the world began the work of revolution at the time when Douglas spoke. And let no answer be attempted, save with recollection of the common tendency of thought, in strong and thoughtful minds, at that time, with reference to the apparent destiny of free opinions in America.

It was not Douglas first, or Douglas only, to whom a patriotic prophecy was ever whispering, that

"The whole boundless continent is ours!"

The people fully felt, and still the people fully feel, the sentiment of Douglas in the language under criticism, if that language be interpreted upon the supposition that the speaker gave expression to the utmost that he meant. In 1852, it seemed to many that our legislator had meant a little more than he expressed. It then appeared to many that the "Little Giant" had been not only willing that irregularity should throttle Cuban oppression and misrule, but that his influence should hasten the deliverance of Cuba through the filibusters.

Willingness to see the unavoidable accomplished suddenly, may still appear to be the *animus* of Douglas at the time alluded to, but we shall find hereafter reason to conclude that want of moderation is the only charge that can be brought with firmness and with confidence against the Oregon and Texas speeches of our legislator.

When our hero entered Congress, he "found upon the statute-book the evidence of a policy to adjust the slavery question and avoid sectional agitation by a geographical line drawn across the continent, separating free territory from slave territory."[3] He "examined the question when the proposition was made for the annexation of Texas in 1845, and though . . . . unable to vindicate the policy of a geographical line, ... not only acquiesced in and supported the measure then, but . . . . did it with the avowed purpose of continuing

[3] Speech of March 22, 1858.

that line to the Pacific Ocean, so soon as we should acquire that territory."[4]

Such is the assurance given by Douglas, and no student of his life can fairly doubt his statement that he merely acquiesced in an established policy, even when he voted for extending the geographical line. He voted, so he tells us, out of the consideration "that the policy had its origin in patriotic motives, in fraternal feeling, in that brotherly affection which ought to animate all the citizens of a common country; and that for the sake of peace, and harmony, and concord, we ought to adhere to and preserve that policy."[5]

The impromptu war speech of our hero[6] in response to Mr. Delano was masterly. It was not moderate—who could be moderate when openly elected representatives openly denounced the war in which our country was engaged as "unholy, unrighteous, and damnable?" When, on the one hand, even venerable Adams "endorsed" and "approved" such language—when, on the other hand, the country was on fire with patriotic expectation—when the weakness and the wickedness of Mexico had opened an apparent way to the expansion of our interests and the development and application of our principles—could there be moderation in the speech of Douglas? Have the consequences of that war been evil? Is the difficulty of the present time its evil consequence? Are we so poor and feeble, that we shrink from the encounter with the questions due to our victorious chastisement of Mexican insolence, and our triumphant annexation of Mexican territory? Are our liberties so worthless that we cannot meet for them and for their permanence the perils of the present conflict

[4] Speech of March 22, 1858. [5] Ib. [6] Delivered May 13, 1846.

of ideas? Even if a conflict bloodier than any known to history should follow that mere moral conflict in which we are now engaged, is he a worthy citizen, is he a real patriot, is he a veritable democrat, who even now can mourn the war with Mexico?

The speech of Douglas, set to martial music by the times in which it sounded to the onset, boldly challenged all the forms of opposition to the cause in which it did such service. It will stand in history as part of the achievements of our arms in Mexico—for arms are nothing if the soldier be not cheered to battle.

It is curious to study how the first experiences of Douglas as a legislator opened the bright pathway for his subsequent career.

The House having before it the substance of Mr. Douglas' amendment to the Wilmot proviso, Mr. Douglas said, that "he believed it was well known that he was against the incorporation of the Wilmot proviso into this bill.[7] And in the second place, that if it should be thought best that the question in regard to the character of new territory to be received thereafter into the Union should be settled now, the most proper arrangement would be the adoption of the Missouri Compromise Line. As the issue now seemed, however, to be on the adoption or the rejection of the Wilmot proviso, he should give a few reasons why he should vote against it. He believed that this was not the proper time for any action on that subject."

It is evident, that there was conflict in the mind of Douglas

7 The Wilmot proviso is too well known to require description. It provided in effect that all newly acquired territories should be non-slaveholding.

as to which of two opinions ought to be adopted—whether it should be believed that Congress ought to act upon the subject of slavery in the territories, or whether the right of acting on that subject was to be attributed to the people of the territory. How he was inclined to choose between these contending ideas, may be indicated by the sentences which follow:

"If Congress should insert no prohibition of slavery in the territorial government, the people of the territory when it became a State or States, could decide for themselves whether slavery should or should not exist within their boundaries. If they chose to prohibit it, and inserted such a feature in their constitution, that constitution must also come before Congress for revision, and Congress might assent or dissent to the provision. *Then the question would be fairly up, and that would be another opportunity of passing upon it, for all future time.*"

I have not imitated those historians of Douglas who appear to be afraid that this speech of our "Little Giant" may reveal that he is not a demi-god.

If Jefferson and Jackson, Clay and Webster, had to learn the way to certainty and truth through doubt and error, shall we presume to make our "Little Giant" an omniscience, an infallibility?

The doctrine *now* to be accepted, it is easy to define. The territorial condition, when it is that of the real immigrant—when it shows the presence of a people, *bona fide*—is now quite evidently far more qualified to furnish its own laws of development than Congress for a long time has been, and than Congress ever will again become. But the reverence of Douglas for the fathers did not suffer him to see this truth, when he delivered the hasty speech,[8] of which a few sentences have been presented to the reader. Was he censurable, in this respect?

A writer of a genius so complete that we must mourn to find it sometimes in the service of extreme opinions, lately wrote: "After all that is said about independent thought, isn't the fact, that a just and good soul has thus or thus believed, a more respectable argument than many that are often adduced? If it be not, more's the pity—since two-thirds of the faith in the world is built on no better foundation."

It was only after this very same great genius had contributed so largely—so unhappily—to agitate the passions and to blind or dazzle the perceptions of the people in respect to slavery, that Douglas ventured fully to accept the mission of propagating, planting, and defending a new development of the principle of popular discretion, or, in other words, of sovereignty. Who will not honor hesitation when it has its source in reverence?

8 Congressional Globe, and Appendix, 1847, p. 440. Mr. Douglas began by desiring "to occupy a portion of the brief space remaining," etc.

CHAPTER II.

THE SENATOR.—FROM '47 TO '54.

As our history advances, the availability of mere allusion and of simple reference increases.

Who is now to learn that, having been elected several times as "Representative in Congress," Douglas was a Senator before he reached the age of thirty-four? Who is to learn that as if in mere anticipation of his Senatorial career, he had been charged as representative with the same committee duty which distinguishes his name to-day far more than all the rest of his career? Who needs to be informed that "as chairman of the Committee on Territories, first in the House and afterward in the Senate, he reported and carried through the bills organizing the Territories of Minnesota, Oregon, New Mexico, Utah, Washington, Kanzas, and Nebraska, and also the bills for the admission into the Union of the States of Iowa, Wisconsin, California, Minnesota, and Oregon?"[1]

The facts enumerated seem enough to fill the glory of that pale-faced emigrant, who tottered towards Winchester in 1833 to find employment as a teacher. Let fanatics question—let

[1] Living Representative Men, 221.

æsthetics sneer—the glory of a life like that which rose from a beginning such as we have contemplated makes it quite impossible for fortune to play tyrant with our hero. Be he chosen or rejected next November, he has been elected to a place in history which the severest censure of his quite unquestionable errors cannot rob of that true lustre found in real greatness.

In addition to the services performed by Douglas in Committee, and the proofs of his administrative powers thus attested, oratory worthy of the Senate has conferred upon the history of that same anxious emigrant to Illinois a lasting and an enviable fame.

Nor, though the gradual development of his so often ridiculed but never to become ridiculous "Great Principle," in Territorial conditions, has engaged so much of the ability of Douglas, has our Senator been a one-ideaed Legislator.

Not alone the Government of Territories within the Union, but the honorable gain of regions not a part of our original domain, has been an object of the patriotic labors by which Douglas is distinguished. We have seen already something of the Douglas tendency in this behalf.

And here the duty of a voter calls upon me to acknowledge that there have been times when greater moderation would have added to the force of argument, and taken from the danger of suggestion, in the speeches of our Senator. There was, or seemed to be some reason, in 1852, to fear that Douglas had not duly frowned upon unlawful movements looking towards Cuba. Frankly, I conceive, that Douglas did not always thoroughly consider oratoric duty when he spoke of territorial expansion. In the main, he aimed at that which all just thinkers will approve. To him, the value of our institutions was forever placed above the reach of doubt. "How am I what I am"—he might have asked—"but through the value of those institutions? Douglas, in the Senate, once went westward, weak, unfriended, and moneyless. Other institutions might have given me a patron and a place—the institutions of this land instead of the placeman's patron have given me the people, and enabled me to feel that in the people's thorough confidence is the most honorable dignity and the most valuable place. In all that crowns my name with reputation, in the offices which I have held, in the great trust confided to me now, appears the value of the democratic principle." And he who could have used such language may be well excused if he has not looked frowningly enough on movements anticipating time in the attempt to join that Cuba which is naturally part of our domain to our expanding territory. At least, such language as the following has given us the right to acquit Douglas of any serious defect of duty in respect to the matter now under consideration:

"This is a government of law. Let us stand by the laws so long as they stand upon the statute book, and execute them faithfully, whether we like or dislike them.

"Sir, I have no fancy for this system of filibustering. I believe its tendency is to defeat the very object in view, to wit, the extension of the area of freedom and the American flag. The President avows that his opposition to it is because it prevents him from carrying out a line of policy that would absorb Nicaragua and the countries against which these expeditions are fitted out. I do not know that I should dissent from the President in that object. I would like to see the boundaries of this Republic extended gradually and steadily as fast as we can Americanize the countries we acquire, and make their inhabitants loyal

American citizens when we get them. Faster than that I would not desire to go."[2]

It may seem that the anti-British oration of Mr. Douglas is not exactly in the Christian spirit. But was it not true that "England does not love us;" did it not seem true "that she cannot love us;" was it not undeniable that "we do not love her either?" Douglas, whose language I have just partly quoted, believed that he spoke truth in saying this and more.[3] Nor can we disagree with him unqualifiedly. We may consider that in literature, England has begun to be more liberal towards America—we may consider that our American development of English thought, combining, as it does, the tributes of the lively, versatile, and yet substantial Irish, of the humanic,

[2] Speech in the Senate, January 7, 1858. See also the speech in which Douglas pronounces our territorial expansion as certain as the continuance of the republic, but adds: "Sir, I am not desirous of hastening the day. I am not impatient of the time when it shall be realized. I do not wish to give any additional impetus to our progress. We are going fast enough. But I wish our policy, our laws, our institutions, should keep up with the advance in science, in the mechanic arts, in agriculture, and in every thing that tends to make us a great and powerful nation. Let us look the future in the face, and let us prepare to meet that which cannot be avoided. Hence, I was unwilling to adopt that clause in the treaty guaranteeing that neither party would ever annex, colonize, or occupy any portion of Central America." Speech of March 10, 1853.

[3] "I cannot go as far as the Senator from South Carolina. I cannot recognize England as our mother. If so, she is, and ever has been a cruel and unnatural mother. I do not find the evidence of her affection in her watchfulness over our infancy, nor in her joy and pride at our ever-blooming prosperity and swelling power, since we assumed an independent position.

"The proposition is not historically true. Our ancestry were not all of English origin. They were of Scotch, Irish, German, French, and of Norman descent, as well as English. In short, we inherit from every branch of the Caucasian race. It has been our aim and policy to profit by their example—to reject their errors and follies—and to retain, imitate, cultivate, perpetuate all that was valuable and desirable. So far as any portion of the credit may be due to England and to Englishmen—and much of it is—let it be freely awarded and recorded in her ancient archives, which seem to have been long since forgotten by her, and the memory of which her present policy towards us is not well calculated to revive." Speech of March 17, 1853

philosophical, trustworthy German, and of its other known constituents, is teaching England her long-needed lesson—we may hope for peace and even for a hearty friendship with the English people—but we must agree in substance, even now, with all that Douglas said a little more than seven years ago. And England must do justice to the country whence so large a tribute is derived to our own population ere, with real warmth, we take the pledge of friendship with the British nationality.

Some of our public men have apparently been of Mickey Free's opinion, when he sung:

> "It's little for glory I care;
> Sure, renown is only a fable."

But the whole weight of authority—the testimony of national behavior and the solemn judgment of the jurists here agreeing—is that "the glory of a nation is intimately connected with its power, and indeed, forms a considerable part of it."[4]

Of this opinion Mr. Douglas, fairly tried with reference to *all* that we have seen of him in this review of his career, approves himself. Believing in him as, some years ago, I did not dream of finding reason to believe in him, I close my glance at his relation to our intercourse with other nations, by submitting that our hero, as a legislator in the period here examined, as well as in the whole of his career since his eclipse,[5] has understood the real glory of America, and nobly labored to promote that interest of nations.

[4] "It is this brilliant advantage that procures it the esteem of other nations, and renders it respectable to its neighbors. A nation whose reputation is well established—especially one whose glory is illustrious—is courted by all sovereigns: they desire its friendship, and are afraid of offending it. Its friends, and those who wish to become so, favor its enterprises, and those who envy its prosperity are afraid to show their ill-will." Vattel, Law of Nations, B. I., ch. 15.

[5] Ante, p. 12.

By the glory of America, the writer means that "true glory which Vattel defines as consisting in "the favorable opinion of men of wisdom and discernment;" which is acquired not by a spirit of unscrupulous aggrandizement, but "by the virtues or good qualities of the head and the heart, and by great actions which are the fruit of those virtues." Read with care the early history of Douglas. Ascertain to what in the bebinning of his wonderful career he devoted what he evidently then regarded as his destiny. Consider what conceivable interest he had at that important period to choose to be a demagogue rather than a democrat. Examine with the utmost care all recent exhibitions of the ripened tendencies of Douglas. As to the interval between the periods thus brought together, scrutinize, with even an unfriendly scrutiny, the words, the bearing, all that has been known and all that could be fairly thought of Douglas. The result is certain. You must own, that the Jacksonian boy has imitated Jackson in the substance of his conduct; and as the character of Jackson, certainly no faultless character, has long since passed into the constellation of the names in which all real lovers of the real glory of America find objects of exalted contemplation, so will the name of Douglas be an object of like contemplation in the years to come.

With reference to the domestic law of nations, to internal polity, to what is often called political economy, the action of our legislator was, with one or two exceptions, perfectly harmonious with right, not only in reality but in appearance.

Early in the Senatorial career of Douglas, he again directed his attention to Internal Improvements.

Mr. Sheahan—whom I quote with pleasure, and whose book,

although it does not answer the design of this volume, I commend to voters—writes:

"Mr. Douglas, during his entire political life, has agreed with the Democratic party in resisting any general system of internal improvements by the federal government. . . . . . Upon some points, however, such as the improvements of rivers and harbors, he has had opinions somewhat peculiar. He has endeavored to discriminate between those works which were essential to the protection of commerce and the improvement of the navigable waters of the country, and those other works asked for by parties having local interests to serve, and desirous to promote them at the expense of the federal treasury. Mr. Douglas voted pretty generally for all the River and Harbor Appropriation Bills, always protesting against such items as were included in them that did not come up to his idea of justice or propriety."

Mr. Douglas felt authorized, in 1854, to "repudiate as unreasonable and unjust, all injurious discrimination predicated upon salt water and tidal arguments, and to insist that if the power of Congress to protect navigation has any existence in the Constitution, it reaches every portion of this Union where the water is in fact navigable, and only ceases where the fact fails to exist."[6] Justly reasoning his way to this conclusion, he proposed a system which I have not space to bring before the reader, but which well attests the practicalness and reliableness which from the beginning of this history we have remarked as a distinction of the character we are contemplating.

Equally in harmony with the known doctrines of the democratic party have been all the doctrines of Mr. Douglas when distinctly, clearly, and definitively stated and added by him to what we may designate as the body of his well-considered views.

[6] Letter of Jan. 22, '54, to Gen. Matteson.

Even the doctrine as to Territorial Discretion, Sovereignty, or Self-Government, the views of Douglas as he came to entertain them in the year 1854, and as he has explained them in his speech of last May, may be regarded as in harmony with settled democratic constitutional ideas.

For athough the doctrine of Judge Douglas in the instance just alluded to presents some features which may be considered not yet familiar to the common mind, its substance is and must be democratic doctrine.

It is easy to establish this position. For the purposes of another work, the writer has elaborated what appears to him a statement equally of democratic doctrine and of American first principles of polity—and with the reader's leave, the following extract may serve our present purposes :

"That the question should be seriously entertained, whether the people of the territories have the moral and should have the legal right to imitate the people of the states in making their own laws, must need some explanation. Territorial conditions must peculiarly require the nearness of the power governing to the people governed. Territorial interests peculiarly secure the care, the discrimination, by which all governmental power should be marked. Wherever but a single, honest family of emigrants selects its future home, intending in good faith to abide by that selection, we have a community which has the interest, if not the capacity, to make good laws for governing its members. Congress may have a superior *capacity* to govern that family as it ought to be governed. But the *interest* of the emigrant family to make good laws for its own government is evidently greater than the interest of Congress to provide good laws for the government of that family. For Congress is a body, formed of members representing chiefly interests in local districts, which have no immediate concern with territorial conditions. Congress is, moreover, constituted so that members feel the force of opinion in their respective districts rather than the force of opinion in the emigrant community of territories. The interest of Congress is but the aggregate of the interest of members of Congress. The interest of individual members of Congress has been shown to be remote from the interest of the emigrant family in territories. It follows, that the interest of Congress to govern territorial communities as they ought to be governed is only a remote interest—inferior, at least, to the interest of the territorial community to be well governed.

"If such is a fair statement with reference to the interest of a single family in a territory, it will be strengthened by supposing the presence of several families in the territory. A common concern will soon unite several families, if they can have the necessary communication with each other. In that common concern, we have an interest to subject the developing community to the government of good laws. The community, in other words, has an interest to subject itself to good laws. And this interest grows with the growth of the community. Else, the whole fabric of our government is false. Else, self-government is a delusion everywhere and under every constitution.

"I have thus far spoken only of the *interest* of the community. This, we have sufficiently observed, is an interest to provide itself with good laws.

"Now, let us look into the *capacity* of the infant community to govern itself wisely and efficiently.

"I have conceded, that a superior capacity to govern the territory *may* reside in Congress. But we must be guarded in making any such concession.

"Congress never was, and probably never will be, *in fact*, so constituted as to have, *in fact*, the supposed superior capacity. But we may *imagine* a Congress, which if it ever came to be a reality, would have the supposed superior capacity.

"In practice, Congress has apparently conceded the inferiority of its capacity. Except as it dealt with well settled questions of policy, or questions supposed to be well settled, it has frequently in effect referred the government of the territorial community to that community itself.

"It is to be observed, however, that in supposing in the territorial community a superior capacity, we must suppose an honest, fair purpose on the part of members of the community to develop the community into a state capable of self-government. There must be no supposition of Emigrant Aid Societies, interposing to form the State. There must be no supposition of Border Ruffianism invading the territory, to take violent or fraudulent possession of the infant government. That there has been such an interposition of Emigrant Aid Societies and such an invasion of Border Ruffianism, is little to the purpose. The facts alluded to were the forced fruits of fanaticism. And at last the people of the territory here alluded to, rebuked fanaticism, and recovered their invaded rights. We have the right to suppose the presence in the territory of a population, honestly and fairly purposing to build a state on fit foundations. So supposing, we may well assert, in behalf of such a population, a capacity to govern itself far better than it could be governed by Congress.

"Thus we have alike the interest and the capacity of self-government in territorial communities."

It may be urged, however, that the territories, "purchased by the common blood and treasure of the Union," ought to be developed only into such a *statehood* as the interests of other States determine. Douglas here would answer that if a republican development freely and fairly take place in any territory, no external interest can really be hostile to that development—that the interest of the States already in the Union really require only that the people of each territory should be left perfectly free to form and regulate their institutions in their own way, subject only to the constitution of the United States.

And here the body of the democratic party, and no inconsiderable number of the citizens who mean to vote for Lincoln, are in harmony with Douglas.[7] Whether he is right or wrong — I think that he is wrong — in holding that while Congress

7 See an article in Cincinnati Commercial, July 26, 1860.

may constitutionally confer, it cannot constitutionally *exercise*, the powers which his system would refer to territorial legislatures, does not seem important. For, if it be evident that the superior interest and the superior capacity which I have supposed do really exist in the territorial legislature, principles of government distinctively American require that Congress should not intervene, with its inferior interest and its inferior capacity. And so, without determining to take or to reject the utmost of the Douglas doctrines, democrats in general agree in substance with those doctrines.

Wherefore, then, did the writer in the introduction point to the time between the introduction of the Kanzas bill and the twenty-second day of March, 1858, as a time of eclipse to Douglas?

Before directly answering, I beg the reader to observe that the supposed eclipse does not include the action of our Senator in 1850. The origination of large part of the adjustment then attempted, and especially of that relating to the territories, was the work of Douglas. And he proved his worthiness to act with Clay and Webster, and to be regarded as in impartial history he must appear, namely, as a truly patriotic statesman, by supporting all the measures then adopted.

It was in the Kanzas act, and in that act in the defect of safeguards to the due population of the territory, and to the due freedom of the people emigrating in good faith to Kanzas, that the glory of our Senator suffered the supposed eclipse.

I have already indicated the important misconception of the purposes of Douglas and of his good faith, into which the writer was led by perception of the defect just mentioned, and a somewhat excited observation of the subsequent behavior of our statesman. I have also indicated my belief that that subsequent behavior, though explained and perhaps excused by the action of Douglas in 1857–8, was not entirely free from blame. And now without discussing worn out questions — taking it for granted that all readers know the bloody history enacted on the plains of Kanzas, and the shameful history enacted at the seat of federal administration — I will only say, that Douglas, having frequent opportunities to speak certain needful words for liberty and right in Kanzas, hesitated to express them, and too long postponed that utterance of them by which his glory was so perfectly restored in '58.

Why did he hesitate?

His views of slavery were national as well as rational. He did not, indeed, think as a distinguished thinker and true patriot — Mr. Stephens of Georgia — now appears to think. That statesman lately wrote:

> "The times, as you intimate, do indeed portend evil. But I have no fears for the institution of slavery, either in the Union or out of it, if our people are but true to themselves; true, stable, and loyal to fixed principles and settled policy; and if they are not thus true, I have little hope of any thing good, whether the present Union lasts or a new one be formed. There is, in my judgment, nothing to fear from the 'irrepressible conflict,' of which we hear so much. Slavery rests upon great truths, which can never be successfully assailed by reason or argument. It has grown stronger in the minds of men the more it has been discussed, and it will still grow stronger as the discussion proceeds, and time rolls on. Truth is omnipotent, and must prevail. We have only to maintain the truth with firmness, and wield it aright. Our system rests upon an impregnable basis, that can and will defy all assaults from without. My greatest apprehension is from causes within—there lies the greatest danger. We have grown luxuriant in the exuberances of our well-being and unparalleled prosperity."

No man can read this language, with due respect for its author, and with recollection of theories which have been lately advocated as to races, without perceiving that the anti-slavery fanatic will have rare work to do before accomplishing the utmost of his expectations. But although our hero had, in consequence of his first marriage,[8] narrowly escaped becoming a slaveholder, and although his children were—perhaps are—slaveholders,[9] he probably regarded slavery—he probably regards it now—as jurists have regarded it.

Jurists have considered slavery as always a departure from the law of nature, and as generally violative of that law. But holding property in man to be exceptional, abnormal, and in general evil, jurists have regarded slavery as capable of having legal sanction, and as perfectly entitled to judicial recognition, where, no matter what its origin, it has become established, and the sovereign decides, in his discretion, that its abolition is impolitic.

Supposing Douglas to have so regarded slavery, he might have spoken out for Kanzas more than once. He did not. And he failed in duty when he did not. He went into eclipse when he so failed in duty.

[8] Mr. Douglas was married, April 7, 1847, to Miss Martha D. Martin, daughter of Col. Robert Martin, of Rockingham Co., N. C.

[9] "In 1847, on the day after his marriage, Colonel Martin placed in Mr. Douglas' hands a sealed package of papers. Upon an examination of these papers, Mr. Douglas found among them a deed of certain plantations, including the servants upon them, in the State of Mississippi, which deed vested the title to both lands and servants in him absolutely. He at once, without one moment's hesitation, sought Colonel Martin and returned him the deed, stating that while he was no abolitionist, and had no sympathy with them in their wild schemes and ultra views respecting slavery, yet he was a northern man by birth, education, and residence, and was totally ignorant of that description of property, and as ignorant of the manner and rules by which it should be governed, and was therefore wholly incompetent," etc. Sheahan's Life, 435. See p. 436 for an account of the final disposition of the slaves .

CHAPTER III.

THE SENATOR—FROM '54 TO '60.

It is not pleasant to dwell upon the concession made at the close of our last chapter.

For it was concession and not accusation, on the writer's part, which described the character of Douglas as in eclipse from '54 to '58. The author is so heartily and thoroughly assured of the general fidelity of our hero to the principles, with reference to which even in youth he began to recognize a certain set of duties as his destiny, that every detected fault in Douglas must be mentioned in this volume, not as charge but as admission.

I repeat, it is not pleasant to dwell on the concession here referred to. He is no true patriot, who, having carefully examined the career of Douglas, loves to dwell upon the evidence of the supposed eclipse.

We pass, then, to the scene in which the hidden glory was to reappear.

The twenty-second day of March, 1858, should be commemorated by the friends of Douglas as the 8th of January, 1815, is commemorated by the friends of Jackson.

Such a statement may be looked upon as mere extravagance

—but it is the result of an attentive study of the life and character which we are contemplating.

In the first place, it is not extravagant to say that Stephen Arnold Douglas will be honored after the close of his active participation in affairs—that is to say, perhaps, after he shall have ceased to live—as Andrew Jackson was honored after he had closed his active public service. As even those who were whigs with democratic antecedents now speak of Jackson with a species of veneration, so even those whigs of the present day who leave the democratic party out of opposition to the "Little Giant" will hereafter speak of Douglas with a species of veneration.

And in the second place, it certainly is not extravagant to look on the scene in the Senate on the 22d day of March, 1858, as the day of the restored and permanent renown of Douglas.

Picture to yourself the array of the Administration, the fanatic advocates of novel doctrines of protection, the fanatic advocates of novel doctrines of prohibition, the expectant people, the awaiting Christian world, when Douglas spoke against that mockery of democratic principle, the proposition to admit the pretended State of Kanzas under the false Lecompton Constitution. When the hour of Douglas comes, masses crowd the Senate galleries, "the lobbies, the stairways, and the anterooms." The writers tell us that at "five minutes after five the galleries were empty; in five minutes more they were filled with a brilliant, fashionable, and intelligent array. In the gentlemen's gallery the people were literally walking on each other. They formed a human pyramid reaching up to the windows, on the inside sills of which some persons were fortunate enough to be lifted."

When our Senator appears, applause announces him. In his calm opening, expressing with simplicity the apprehension that his strength of body may prove insufficient for the task before him, we begin to see what he conceived to be the greatness of that task, and we listen with an expectation never given but to greatness. Sentence after sentence warrants and exalts the expectation raised by the first utterance of this immortal speech. Fact follows fact in the statement, vindication after vindication follows in the ever warming argument developed out of that arrangement of related facts. Whoever has doubted Douglas or denounced him, must now believe in his fidelity to his peculiar view of right, and must in that peculiar view of right discern an object of surpassing interest. The life of our American democracy seems breathing in this orator for constitutional interests. Hear him but a little:

"It matters not whether this Constitution is to be the permanent fundamental law of Kanzas, or is to last only a day, or a month, or a year; because, if it is not their act and deed, you have no right to force it upon them for a single day. If you have the power to force it upon this people for one day, you may do it for a year, for ten years, or permanently. The principle involved is the same. It is as much a violation of fundamental principle, a violation of popular sovereignty, a violation of the Constitution of the United States, to force a state Constitution on an unwilling people for a day, as it is for a year or for a longer time. When you set the example of violating the fundamental principles of free government, even for a short period, you have made a precedent that will enable unscrupulous men in future times, under high partisan excitement, to subvert all the other great principles upon which our institutions rest.

"But, sir, is it true that this Constitution may be changed immediately by the people of Kanzas? The President of the United States tells us that the people can make and unmake Constitutions at pleasure; that the people have no right to tie their own hands and prohibit a change of the Constitution until 1864, or any other period; that the right of change always exists, and that the change may be made by the people at any time in their own way, at pleasure, by the consent of the Legislature. I do not agree that the people cannot tie their own hands. I hold that a Constitution is a social compact between all the people of the state that adopts it; between each man in the state, and every other man; binding upon them all; and they have a right to say it shall only be changed at a particular time and in a particular manner, and then only after such and such periods of deliberation. Not only have they a right to do this, but it is wise that the fundamental law should have some stability, some permanency, and not be liable to fluctuation and change by every ebullition of passion."

Is it so that demagogues discourse of constitutions?

Hear our Senator yet further. Do these tones resemble those of one who "went crawling back into a Senatorial caucus as a democrat,"[1] or who ever crawls towards his object, be that object what it may? Have crawlers words like these?—

"For my own part, Mr. President, come what may, I intend to vote, speak, and act according to my own sense of duty so long as I hold a seat in this chamber. I have no defence of my Democracy. I have no professions to make of my fidelity. I have no vindication to make of my course. Let it speak for itself. The insinuation that I am acting with the Republicans or Americans has no terror, and will not drive me from my duty or propriety. It is an argument for which I have no respect. When I saw the Senator from Virginia acting with the Republicans on the Neutrality Laws, in support of the President, I did not feel it to be my duty to taunt him with voting with those to whom he hap-

[1] The allusion is to a recent speech of F. P. Stanton, Esq.

pened to be opposed in general politics. When I saw the Senator from Georgia acting with the Republicans on the Army Bill, it did not impair my confidence in his fidelity to principle. When I see Senators here every day acting with the Republicans on various questions, it only shows me that they have independence and self-respect enough to go according to their own convictions of duty, without being influenced by the course of others.

"I have no professions to make upon any of these points. I intend to perform my duty in accordance with my own convictions. Neither the frowns of power nor the influence of patronage will change my action, or drive me from my principles. I stand firmly, immovably upon those great principles of self-government and state sovereignty upon which the campaign was fought and the election won. I stand by the time-honored principles of the Democratic party, illustrated by Jefferson and Jackson—those principles of state rights, of state sovereignty, of strict construction, on which the great Democratic party has ever stood. I will stand by the Constitution of the United States, with all its compromises, and perform all my obligations under it. I will stand by the American Union as it exists under the Constitution. If, standing firmly by my principles, I shall be driven into private life, it is a fate that has no terrors for me. I prefer private life, preserving my own self-respect and manhood, to abject and servile submission to executive will. If the alternative be private life or servile obedience to executive will, I am prepared to retire. Official position has no charms for me when deprived of that freedom of thought and action which becomes a gentleman and a Senator."

On the following twenty-ninth of April, Douglas thrilled the Senate with these sentences:

"Mr. President, I say now, as I am about to take leave of this subject, that I never can consent to violate that great principle of State equality, of State sovereignty, of popular sovereignty, by any discrimination, either in the one direction or in the other. My position is taken. I know not what its consequences will be personally to me. I will not inquire what those consequences may be. If I cannot remain in public life, holding firmly, immovably, to the great principle of self-government and State equality, I shall go into private life, where I can preserve the respect of my own conscience under the conviction that I have done my duty and followed the principle wherever its logical consequences carried me."

But no such dire result of duty followed, of conviction honored, of true manliness exhibited in an exalted scene of action, was to make the history of Douglas a discouragement to public virtue.

Having in the Senate, up to June, 1858, and since the introduction of the Kanzas bill, devoted a characteristic attention to British Aggression, and otherwise (as is so generally known that it need not be stated here), approved himself a democratic legislator worthy of the name, the destiny of Douglas soon exposed him to a view, in which we plainly see his hold upon the people, and the people's hold on him.

The reader knows that we approach the celebrated contest between Lincoln and our hero.

The continued presence of Douglas in the Senate would depend on the Illinois elections of November, 1858. Douglas was opposed by Lincoln, the latter being substantially backed alike by the so-called Republican Party in Illinois and by the so-called Democratic President at Washington. The eloquent popular addresses made by Lincoln, and the eloquent unpopular appeals made by the administration equally fell short of their design. There was "a Douglas to the rescue," and the victory belonged to real greatness, to the people, in a word, to democratic interests and principles.

In four months, the "Little Giant" made one hundred and thirty speeches, all of them but three delivered in the most unconfined form of the popular assembly. Having no contemptible opponent, he was not perfunctorily ventilating his "great principle." His speeches could not well enhance his reputation—yet they seemed to make new revelations of his strength.

Although suspected of a secret understanding with Republicans, he boldly said in his first campaign speech:

"I will be entirely frank with you. My object was to secure the right of the people of each State and of each Territory, North or South, to decide the question for themselves, to have slavery or not, just as they choose; and my opposition to the Lecompton Constitution was not predicated upon the ground that it was a pro-slavery constitution (cheers), nor would my action have been different had it been a free-soil constitution. . . . . . . I deny the right of Congress to force a slaveholding State upon an unwilling people. (Cheers.) I deny their right to force a free State upon an unwilling people. (Cheers.")

These doctrines, and the cheers with which the democratic audience at Chicago heard them, mark the difference between the democratic tendencies of thought, and those by which the generally good citizens but seldom thorough political reasoners of the republican party are distinguished. Douglas and his democratic audience, whatever they might have chosen with reference to Kanzas and that moment, regarded the whole country and all time too much to sacrifice to Kanzas what belongs to the Union, or to sacrifice to any present interest the permanent interest of constantly attested democratic principles.

Indeed, the opposition to the democratic party, call it as you will, is like all precedent forms of opposition to that party: it conserves a part at the expense of the whole, the present at the expense of the future.

Douglas and his hearers were not unwilling that the South should gain whatever territory could be gained by the fair conservatism and the just observance of the principle, "which asserts the exclusive right of a free people to form and adopt their own fundamental law, and to manage and regulate their own internal affairs and domestic institutions." Lincoln and his hearers would have sacrificed that principle rather than an inch of territory or a moment of apparent triumph to their adversaries.

Whoever reads with care the published speeches—they were not debates—of Stephen Arnold Douglas and of Abraham Lincoln will arise from fair examination of them, with such thoughts as these: Here are two men, of whom one is great and both are true as well as able. Lincoln represents, not greatly, but with marked ability, the least objectionable form of republicanism. Douglas represents, and greatly, the most patriotic form of democracy. Lincoln magnifies the interests of keeping territories now free in that condition, slightly estimating, or forgetting to preserve intact, the principle without which freedom in the territories or elsewhere would be a sheer impossibility. Douglas magnifying nothing, nor depreciating aught, devotes himself to the elucidation and the preservation of the principle on which all real republican or democratic interests must always be dependent.

It is curious (I may observe in passing) to remark, that Mr. Breckenridge and his supporters, though insisting on the interest of slavery, while Mr. Lincoln and his party call for anti-slavery legislation, imitate the latter in preferring present interests to permanent concerns, a present triumph to a lasting victory.

Throughout the Illinois discussion, Douglas takes it for certain, that the Dred Scott case has not precluded him from arguing in favor of his darling doctrine as to territorial discretion. In the platform on which he so worthily appears as the chief representative of the only true rational and national democracy, it is treated as an open question whether, in the case alluded to, the Supreme Court has indicated the measure of restriction imposed by the Federal Constitution on the power of the Territorial Legislature over the subject of the domestic relations. Many of us think—for my part, I am clearly of opinion—that the *dicta* of that case will never be so transformed into the law of binding precedent as to become obligatory on the courts and therefore on the loyal citizen. Before it can become so, judges, even in the highest places, will have learned the meaning of the Constitution as the people understand it. Not in the intemperate discussions of town meetings, not in reckless agitation, not in artificially produced interpretations by the people of the Constitution, will a judge attempt to find the meaning of that instrument. But the judge who ventures to despise the solemn reading, the deliberate construction, of the Constitution by the people, ought to be impeached. His conscience *will* impeach him. For, although he may at last find warrant for adhering to his own construction, it must be quite evident to him, that his construction *may* be violative, not alone of the true significance inherent in a given constitutional provision, but of the sacred principle, that all the forms of law derive their political substance and legal vigor from the will of the people. Is it not important, therefore, that the facts alluded to in the initial sentences of this paragraph—to say nothing of a certain rather strict construction given by Judge Douglas to the *dicta* alluded to—have left our hero free to represent before the people, and the people free to appreci ate in his election or defeat, the interest of the "great principle," to which our hero now devotes his life? If I have not mistaken what is now impending, thought will be appealed to, and deliberation—warmed, it may be, by a patriotic fervor, but still serving reason and expressing judgment—may determine the approaching contest by this reading of the Constitution and this interpretation of the necessary tenets of American democracy: "That every distinct political community, loyal to the Constitution and the Union, is entitled to all the rights, privileges, and immunities of self-government in respect to its local concerns and internal polity, subject only to the Constitution of the United States." If so, no quibble as to the last clause of the preceding sentence[2] will degrade the sanctuary of judicial action, nor will sectional suggestions penetrate the presence of decision by the judges. There will be occasion to remark a restoration and a promise. Constitutional constructions long respected in the courts of justice will be restored. The action of the judges will reveal the promise of the Union to be permanent, and the promise of democracy to make a new manifestation of its fitness as a principle of government.

Triumphing in the local contest, Douglas soon resumed his senatorial position. He again devoted all that in him was to the public service. He again displayed himself as quite

[2] The words are those of Douglas.

unalterably attached, as a statesman, to the principles of the democratic party. Is not this sufficient eulogy, as well as sufficient indication, of the recent course of Douglas in the Senate?

Mr. F. P. Stanton thinks it is not. He objects that "Douglas has not maintained his position to the end." He adds: "After the Democratic party had abandoned its principles, he ought not to have gone to Charleston at all. He should have hoisted the standard of true Democracy, and defied the Charleston Democracy; and this, gentlemen, is what I, in my humble way, advised him to do. He thought different, and wished to purify the party. I told him that they would crush him, and they have done it. They decapitated him for the Chairman of the Committee on Territories, and Senator Green substituted in his place. I thought then he would take my advice, but I was chagrined to find that he didn't meet this outrage as I would have done. You saw that just after that act that Douglas went crawling back into a senatorial caucus as a Democrat—whereas he had only a little while before been kicked out for not being a Democrat."

The chagrin alluded to by Mr. Stanton does not equal that which may be well predicted for him. After trying his philosophy as a republican, perhaps the lesson of the life of Douglas will be understood by Stanton.

In the first place, all the difficulties of our present condition cannot hide the facts of history so well presented recently by one with whom the writer has not always quite agreed, but in whom he always proudly recognizes genius and fidelity to principle. In a recent speech, Senator Pugh well reminds us that "the history of the democratic party is the history of the country. Whatever is great in the history of the country, either in war or peace, is due to that party. It is not infallible, and like all things human, may sometimes fail; but whatever errors it has committed, have been corrected in good time. It is now the only organization capable of maintaining the integrity and stability of the government."

In the next place, Douglas, in the very action which has, perhaps, chagrined his quondam friend into a Lincolnite, attested his determination to restore whatever had been taken from the integrity of the democratic party. He could do it, but he could not do it in contempt of the principle that the means must be adapted to the end. He could not do it by a rash abandonment of his position in the democratic party, and the taking of position with the good men who, although they constitute the numbers, do not exercise the power, of the republican party.

But I will not here further anticipate my view of Douglas as a candidate. I wish to bring to a conclusion my account of Douglas as a legislator.

Faithful to principles which, at the outset, made him a Jacksonian democrat, the whole career of Douglas has, excepting only the eclipse already witnessed, illustrated the completeness and the fitness of Jacksonian principles to govern wisely, to promote the real wealth, to secure the real glory, of such a people as the American Union binds together. In a sketch like that presented to the reader, no detail is possible. But by allusion, reference, or otherwise, I have presented to the reader almost all that I desire to say of Douglas as a Senator.[3]

[3] The speech of May 15 and 16, 1860, will be referred to in our next division—in the view of Douglas as a Candidate.

It is not impertinent to our design to say a word in this connexion of our Senator as he appears in private life.

Without attempting to attract, nay, rather (for here unimportant reasons) wishing to avoid, the special notice of our hero, the writer has encountered Douglas more than once in social conversation. What he has submitted as to pithy sayings, forceful jests, strong answers, and *strong silences*,[4] is partly the result of a direct observation of the characteristics of Douglas. Meeting him at Cincinnati, eight years ago, and at Columbus twice since then, I so observed his "characters" as to imagine that I learned a little of his character. It is not of the Claude Loraine landscape, or the Raphael Madonna, order. Sunday-like, sunshiny geniality is not the indication of our hero's presence or his manner. The æsthetics also, to whom I have before referred as finding their beloved type in Breckinridge, would not discern in Douglas Breckinridge's courtly style. But for a natural, straightforward, goodly, though it be but mortal, fitness for encountering constituents, commend me to Judge Douglas. And for real geniality, and wholesome grace, and forceful dignity, commend me also to our "Little Giant."

Forceful is a word of constantly suggested application to our hero. When I pointed to his forceful jests, I used no unconsidered phrase. It may sometimes appear that in the character of Douglas there is lack of that important element called humor. But there is a real, earnest, forceful humor in that character, of which the forceful jest is often the expression.

Answers of great strength occasionally call for admiration

[4] Ante, p. 44.

in the social intercourse of Douglas. But forceful silences are yet more characteristic of that intercourse.

Of that more inward life of Douglas, which reveals the charm of home,[5] I am not able to inform the reader. But if all we read be true, the eclipse recorded by the writer must have been after all only partial. It was during that eclipse that Douglas formed his present conjugal relation—and all accounts of Mrs. Douglas celebrate her loveliness.

[5] Senator Douglas having lost the wife already mentioned, was married to his present wife, Miss Adele Cutts, Nov. 20, 1856.

THE CANDIDATE.

8

CHAPTER I.

THE CANDIDATE FOR FORENSIC OFFICE.

ONLY two forensic offices have been held by Douglas—that of State's Attorney and that of Judge.

To each of these offices, he was elected by the Legislature. But with reference to each, the popularity which Douglas from the very first of his experience in Illinois began to acquire, must be considered. So that we might in the present chapter take that suppletory view of Douglas as a candidate which is in order in the present division of this work.

But I prefer to make the purposed further observation of the popularity of Douglas, in the chapters which relate to the Candidate for Legislative Office and the Candidate for the Presidency.

I conclude this brief chapter, therefore, by the statement that we have no evidence of over-anxiety on the part of Douglas as a candidate for forensic office. On the contrary, the judgeship was not sought by him.

CHAPTER II.

THE CANDIDATE FOR LEGISLATIVE OFFICE.

WHEN Douglas left New England to become a Western man, the way was well opened to him, as we have already seen, to understand two important principles of the true American political system.

One of these, as we have also seen, related to the very constitution of the people, to the population of this scene of the combination, modification, and development of national peculiarities. The other, we have also ascertained, relates to the political and social conflict and harmony of the varieties in religious faith.

The first asserted it to have been, and to continue to be, the right of humanity itself—of man as man—to people this New World with tributes from the population of the Old World, and their derivatives. The second asserted the duty of government in this new scene of national development to establish social and political equality among the varieties of religious faith.

It was understood by the democratic party of the time of Jefferson, and it was a part of the Jacksonian version or development of the Jeffersonian constitutional democracy, that the native and adopted citizen, without distinction of religious faith, must equally participate in the right of suffrage and the right of being represented in the moulding of our laws and the administration of our public justice.

Either in a distinctive manner of expressing the principles just recognized, or in a distinctive heartiness in their acceptance, the followers of Jefferson and Jackson won the preference in general of citizens whose place of birth was transatlantic. Those opposed to Jefferson and Jackson, consequently, grew unfriendly to the "foreign element."

It followed that to be, as Douglas was, a Jacksonian democrat, was to find attached and loyal friends; and these our hero found.

From the first, indeed, all circumstances tended to attract to Douglas public confidence in Illinois. That walk to Winchester—a walk which certain recollections force the writer to regard with a peculiar interest—was a valuable introduction of our hero to the people among whom he was to live and to be a candidate.

Arrived at Winchester,[1] the service which our young adventurer to western possibilities of fame and fortune rendered to the auctioneer, variously prefigured our hero's subsequent career.

The accuracy of his service, and its nameless indication of capacity for higher service, attracted such a notice to young Douglas as prefigured his selection for forensic office, for Committee duty in and out of legislative bodies, and the like.

The conversation during intervals of the three days' employment here referred to was the next prefiguration of the subse-

[1] Ante, p. 45.

quent career of Douglas. It was chiefly political. The young Jacksonian[2] knew the principles of that development of Jeffersonian democracy which dates from Jackson. What he knew of Jackson made him an enthusiast of principles, themselves attractive to a thorough thinker. He explained, defended, illustrated, advocated the Jacksonian democracy.

His conversation, and the confidence in Douglas which resulted from it, plainly enough prefigure our hero at the bar and on the stump, in popular assemblies and in Senatorial debate. In its manner, as we may suppose the latter, it prefigures Douglas as an orator.[3]

And it is easy to discern another prefiguration of Douglas' subsequent career. Knowing what this history has shown of our candidate—what some of us have learned of him in public or in private audience—what no fair-minded voter will deny to him—we have the right to add, that the strong sense and practical, reliable, as well as ample knowledge shown by the auctioneer's assistant, made him arbiter and judge as well as advocate.

The whole effect, indeed, of these three days of accidental service, accidental conversation with the people, accidental acquirement of the germ of popularity, was another prefiguration of the subsequent career of Douglas. That effect deserves the name of a success. Our hero was befriended so generally and so promptly that his school of forty pupils, "started" in November, '33, enabled him in '34, to hang his shingle, and to enter regularly on the practice of the law.

The fact, already mentioned, that our hero did not study the effect of dress, must not mislead us into the supposition that

[2] Ante, p. 34. [3] Ante, p. 44. See also page 60.

he was inaccurate or unreliable in drawing papers for his clients, pleadings for the record, or the like. The history of special pleaders quite forbids this supposition, as all lawyers know. To mention but two instances, very different, indeed, we may name the English Chief Justice Saunders (pah! there is a stench in his mere memory!) and our Chief Justice Parsons. These and other well known instances being considered in connexion with the indications furnished by the volumes of reports already mentioned, we may easily account for the early selection of Douglas as the candidate of the democratic party for representative in the Legistature of Illinois.

He had served, the reader will remember, as State's Attorney.

To these suggestions, we must add that of the popularity acquired by Douglas, by drawing and presenting the resolutions at a Jackson meeting, and by his victory over a politician, "name of" Lamborn. Douglas' triumph caused him to be crowed over as a "High-Combed Cock," as well as a "Little Giant" on that memorable occasion.[4]

What was the peculiar style of speaking by which Douglas won his first distinction as a stumper, we can only guess.

It is quite probable that he was then as now distinguished by the use of language easily intelligible to all hearers. Mr. Milburn, more than twenty years ago, remarked our candidate's "first-hand knowledge of the people"—his acquaintance with the popular ideas, and his familiarity with the language of the people in expressing these ideas.[5]

Lately, it has been objected that our candidate is too monot-

[4] Sheahan's Life, 19.

[5] Ante, p. 60.

onous—that he manifests in his speaking not the least appreciation of the mountains, plains, and valleys, seas, and lakes and rivers, trees, and shrubs, and flowers, in which other orators find illustrations and conceits.

Monotony is hardly to be found in Douglas' speeches. He, indeed, repeats, reiterates, insists upon the principle which he deems fundamental, and which is so, in our political system. Here he manifests, not ignorance, but knowledge, of his personal interests and the interests of that which he considers as his cause.

But space will not allow the writer to discuss the question whether Douglas is an orator. Opponents always find him one, wherever and whenever they oppose him.

The faith of Douglas in the principle (which might now be defined as an article of the democratic creed)[6]—"that every distinct political community, loyal to the Constitution and the Union, is entitled to all the rights, privileges and immunities of self-government in respect to its local concerns and internal polity, subject only to the Constitution of the United States," was not well defined at the time when he was first a candidate for legislative office. Perhaps, I ought to say, that at that time, neither Douglas nor any other person saw the applicability of this principle to territorial communities. For, after all, the principle, simply stated as we have just employed the words of Douglas to express it, would always have commanded the assent of democratic minds. The trouble was, we had not learned that a territorial community must necessarily be a "distinct political community"—a people, which, "if loyal to the Constitution and the Union," should be regarded as having

[6] Ante, p 116

the interest and the capacity[7] which constitute the right of self-government.

But while our candidate had not yet seen the entire applicability of his principle, in common with all democrats of the Jacksonian school, he believed its substance, and it was to him as a political religion.

This it was that made him so often and so soon a successful candidate for the trust and dignity of legislative office. For whoever doubts the principle of popular discretion, popular self-government, the people do not doubt it.

Douglas may not be well read in what they call political economy. What statesman ever learned to legislate from being well read in that branch of "science?" But Douglas is well read in that instructive book, the people. Understanding what he reads in that direction, he has easily acquired his great distinction as a statesman. Having found the key to the difficulties of political economy,[8] he has opened them in presence of the people, and the people have confided in their representative.

7 Ante, p. 93.

8 Ante, p. 78.

CHAPTER III.

THE CANDIDATE FOR THE PRESIDENCY.

Of the Presidential candidate in 1852 and in 1856, I have already intimated all that I desire to say.

I hasten to a view of Douglas, in which he appears before us as a present candidate for the Supreme Political Distinction in America.

He so appears as repesenting a recent expression of the principles maintained by the deliberate convictions of the people.

This expression asserts, among other things, as Douglas constantly asserts, the principle now known as Popular Sovereignty. In Douglas, then, we find the representative of a great truth or a great fallacy.

I have attempted to establish that our candidate is not devoted to a fallacy. Since what I wrote, with that design, was printed, I have read an article by Mr. Brownson,[1] which endeavors to establish that the tenet of Popular Sovereignty as held by Douglas and his party tends to filibusterism, to the election of judges by the people and the consequent destruction

1 Art. "Politias at Home," Brownson's Review, July, 1860.

of judicial freedom, purity and dignity, as well as to other mobocratic evils.

It is worthy of remark, that if this objection be well taken, our whole system lacks foundation, or in other words, is based upon a fallacy. If the exercise of the right of self-government tends to the election of judges by the people, and if the election of judges by the people tends to judicial constraint, corruption, degradation, let us give up the suicidal right of self-government at once. If the exercise of the same right tends to filibusterism, and filibusterism tends to international as well as domestic anarchy, let us at once reform the constitution.[2]

Fair comparison, however, of the conservatism with which a constitutional democracy associates its tendency to progress and experiment, will show it to be more reliable than that which anti-democratic principles would furnish as the safeguard of our liberties. Whoever, after due reflection, holds that this opinion is a fallacy, must also hold that our whole governmental system is a fallacy.

There is, undoubtedly, a difficulty to be encountered in the maintenance of the "great principle" of Mr. Douglas. But it is not that which we have just encountered.

The extremists of the South may tell us: Douglas does not think, and those among his followers who are non-slaveholders do not think, that slavery is a blessing—that the constitution

[2] It is also worthy of remark in passing, that the learned and able reviewer has himself assailed, not only the mere *dicta*, but the binding, precedental point of the decision in the Dred Scott case. Now, unfortunately for his argument, this most unhappy of all infelicitous decisions, this most political of all political decisions, was not made by judges elected by the people, but by judges appointed, and to hold their offices while they shall well behave!

carries property in man like property in horses into all the territories of the Union—and we cannot trust a man who fails in these particulars. And the extremists of the North may tell us: Douglas will not shriek with us against the crying sin, and desolating curse, and unutterable abomination, of man-holding.

How Douglas must encounter such a difficulty as this, we have already partly seen.

To each of the objectors, however, he might, and probably he would, thus answer: I regard slavery as all men of sense before long will once more regard it. Looking on it as it is a Kentucky, a Virginia, or a Mississippi legal institution, I have really little to say or think about it. If I think of it at all as such an institution of a sovereign State, I do not find that it has added to the number of slaves in the world, and I do find that it has mitigated the rigor of enslavement to those who were already slaves. Not being a citizen of a slave State, it has not been my duty to study, as it ought to be studied if at all, the question how, and when, or whether at any time, the interest of master and slave, or the real interest of either, may require the legal dissolution of the relation involved in slavery. As for the slavery question as it may arise in territories, you have learned my views. If the Constitution, as finally interpreted by the Supreme Court, do not forbid the people of the territories to govern themselves in reference to slavery, the extension or non-extension of slavery in the territories shall be determined, not by Presidents or Congresses, but by the communities, the peoples, chiefly and directly interested in the subject-matter.

But, it may be asked, if Douglas were a territorian, how would he vote respecting slavery?

I do not know. But, voter! let us try to guess.

I guess, then, that before deciding, Douglas as a territorian would try to understand. He would examine the opinions of Calhoun—a great good man—in favor of the Christianity, in other words of the humaneness, of slavery in America. He would examine the opinions of that Alexander Stephens, whose opinions have been glanced at in this volume, and of others, South, and the opinions of a Corwin and a Thayer, North. And, finally, before deciding he would study latitude and longitude, and pay a due attention to those mountains, valleys, and plains, those seas, and lakes, and rivers, and those trees, and shrubs, and flowers, which it has been said his oratory fails to notice and to illustrate. How after all, he would decide, it may be difficult even to guess. But if he thinks, as I believe he does, that slavery, although it may be unobjectionable where it is, would *generally* be objectionable in a territory free from it at present, how he would determine generally needs no indication.

These, the reader will observe, are my conjectures, not the words of Douglas. I have not been authorized by Douglas to write a single line of this volume—not a line of it has been submitted to him—not a line of it must charge any one but the writer himself.

If an inordinate ambition cannot be shown in Douglas—it is charged against him—we may well conclude, that our candidate is well worthy of the high position lately given to him by the action of his party.

No inordinate ambition touched the lips of Douglas as with a supernal fire when he defeated the Lecompton Constitution.

No inordinate ambition showed itself in Douglas when he said: "I prefer the position of Senator, or even that of a private citizen, where I would be at liberty to defend and maintain the well defined principles of the democratic party, to accepting a presidential nomination upon a platform incompatible with the princple of self-government in the territories, or the reserved rights of the States, or the perpetuity of the Union under the Constitution." [7]

No, there is no inordinate ambition in the man who utters language such as this—and proves by conduct that he means precisely what his language signifies.

What, then, are we to pronounce respecting Douglas?

Clearly stating, boldly uttering, reiterating in all presences, the doctrine, that the people may be trusted with all political questions; fully, nobly, gloriously redeemed, if ever he has erred as we believe; the ablest and the most distinguished living statesman, true to our American system in its integrity; our Candidate seems well entitled to the Presidency.

The æsthetics under Breckenridge may not admire him. The believers in extreme opinions, North and South, may anxiously endeavor to defeat the people's real choice. They may succeed. The people may be kept from seeing Douglas as he is. But they who know him, even if they do not think him faultless, find in him a thorough fitness for the Presidency which they think cannot fairly be attributed to any other candidate.

Here I must bring to a conclusion this imperfect, but I trust impartial Version of the Life and Character of Douglas.

In addition to the views of our Candidate in the Senate,

[7] See also the quotation on page 102.

which we have already taken, I would like to give an outline of the speech of last May. In this speech Douglas vindicates his record, shows the national and rational character of his democracy, proves that he deserves to be accepted at whatever cost of self-correction in the North, the South, the East, the West, throughout the Union. But I must refer the reader to the speech itself—I have not space to give its outline.

Before concluding, I would also gladly follow Douglas through his European travel, observation, conversation, presentation and failure to be presented. But I must only thus glance at the Old World observation and experience of our Candidate.

Yet a word or two, and I will leave my hero to that "destiny," of which he speaks so often.

From the very nature of this undertaking, there could be but little novelty in its account of Douglas as a private individual. No intimacy on the part of the writer with Douglas has supplied the former with rich or various materials for this production. But the people have but little now to learn, of that which they have properly a right to know, of Stephen Arnold Douglas. For, the "Little Giant" has been so abused in body and in mind—with reference to his peculiar stretch of legs as well as his peculiar reach of understanding—in his habits of the body and in his habits of the mind—that the absurd attempts of foolish enemies to injure him have served him well before the people. In the very desperation of these pitiful attacks, there is a plain confession of the strength of Douglas. And assaults of this description only serve to make the people more attentively observe the marked peculiarities of the well designated "Little Giant." On the other hand, the nickname just applied to Douglas has for years attested the familiar and affectionate regard with which the masses early learned to look upon "the Senator from Illinois." And this regard itself was due to traits of character in our hero which no manufactured reputation, and no artificial greatness, ever equaled in attracting the affection of the people.

Here submitting my production to the reader's judgment and his conscience, what shall I anticipate of its reception by the public? Nothing. All I know with certainty about it is, that it has been designed for usefulness. Whether it shall be confined in its reception to a narrow circle of unfavorable critics, or shall at the best be circulated in a little sphere of friendly toleration, or, commended by its dedication to the truth, shall bear a message of good will to distant latitudes, it were vain to speculate. I leave this little volume to that Providence which often makes the most ambitious efforts agents of humiliation, and which sometimes seems to work the greatest good with the least considerable instruments.

INDEX.

[1] In the text, I omitted to refer to the bold and manly speeches of Mr. Douglas against Know Nothingism—in favor of true and against false Americanism.

www.ingramcontent.com/pod-product-compliance
Lightning Source LLC
LaVergne TN
LVHW021416110826
845150LV00007B/1957

* 9 7 8 1 4 2 5 5 0 9 2 5 5 *